Acting Out

Understanding and Reducing Aggressive Behaviour in Children and Youth

Editor: David A. Wolfe

camh
Centre for Addiction and Mental Health

A Pan American Health Organization /
World Health Organization
Collaborating Centre

Library and Archives Canada Cataloguing in Publication

Acting out: understanding and reducing aggressive behaviour in children and youth / editor, David A. Wolfe.

Includes bibliographical references.

ISBN: 978-0-88868-532-2 (PRINT)
ISBN: 978-0-88868-587-2 (PDF)
ISBN: 978-0-88868-588-9 (HTML)
ISBN: 978-0-88868-890-3 (ePUB)

1. Acting out (Psychology). 2. Aggressiveness in children. 3. Aggressiveness in adolescence. I. Wolfe, David A. II. Centre for Addiction and Mental Health

RJ506.A35A24 2007   155.4'18232   C2006-905567-X

Printed in Canada

This publication may be available in other formats. For information about alternative formats or other CAMH publications, or to place an order, please contact Sales and Distribution:
Toll-free: 1 800 661-1111
Toronto: 416 595-6059
E-mail: publications@camh.ca
Online store: http://store.camh.ca

Website: www.camh.ca

This book was produced by CAMH's Knowledge and Innovation Support Unit.

2888 / 02-2013 / PY024

Contents

About the editor

David A. Wolfe, PhD, holds the inaugural RBC Chair in Children's Mental Health at the Centre for Addiction and Mental Health (CAMH). He is a Professor of Psychiatry and Psychology at the University of Toronto and Head of the CAMH Centre for Prevention Science. David has broad research and clinical interests in abnormal child and adolescent psychology, with a special focus on child abuse, domestic violence and developmental psychopathology. He and his colleagues (Peter Jaffe, Claire Crooks and Ray Hughes) are currently evaluating "The Fourth R," a comprehensive school-based initiative for reducing adolescent violence and related risk behaviours through the promotion of positive, non-violent relationships.

David is the 2005 recipient of the Canadian Psychological Association's Donald O. Hebb Award for Distinguished Contributions to Psychology as a Science. He is Editor-in-Chief of *Child Abuse & Neglect: The International Journal*. His recent books include *Adolescent Risk Behaviors: Why Teens Experiment and Strategies to Keep Them Safe* (with Peter Jaffe and Claire Crooks; Yale University Press, 2006); *Child Abuse: Implications for Child Development and Psychopathology*, 2nd edition (Sage, 1999); and *Abnormal Child Psychology*, 3rd edition (with Eric Mash; Wadsworth, 2005).

Acknowledgments

Many CAMH clinicians in the Child, Youth and Family Program contributed their breadth of knowledge and practical experience to the development of this book. Their guidance and input shaped the content and forms the core of the book.

Drafts were reviewed by people with scientific or clinical expertise about the topic and by people who are the intended audience for the publication.

Project manager
Margaret Kittel Canale, M.Ed., CAMH

Writers
Anita Dubey, B.Sc., BAA
Karen Shenfeld, BA

CAMH Child, Youth and Family Program Contributors
Lindley Bassarath, MD, FRCPC, Staff Psychiatrist; Assistant Professor, University of Toronto
Gloria Chaim, MSW, RSW, Deputy Clinical Director
Janine DeRosie, Child and Youth Worker
Lew Golding, MA, Manager, Substance Abuse Program for African Canadian and Caribbean Youth (SAPACCY)
Umesh Jain, MD, PhD, Assistant Professor, University of Toronto
Sherri MacKay, PhD, C.Psych., Provincial Director, The Arson Prevention Program for Children (TAPP-C); Assistant Professor of Psychiatry, University of Toronto
Joanne Shenfeld, MSW, RSW, Service Manager, Youth and Family Addiction Programs
Tracey Skilling, PhD, C.Psych., Staff Psychologist; Assistant Professor, University of Toronto

Toronto District School Board Contributor
Stephanie Karatsu, BA, B.Ed., Special Education Teacher, CAMH

Reviewers
Debbie Chiodo, CAMH Centre for Prevention Science
Jennifer Edward, Teacher, York Region District School Board
Marla Glass, Teacher, Toronto District School Board
Marita Granholm, School Child and Youth Worker, Spring Program, Children's Aid Society of the District of Thunder Bay
Gail Hamelin, BSW, MSW, Social Worker and Supervisor, Family Services, Kinark Child and Family Services
Mary Lawand, Special Education Teacher (retired)
Lynn MacKay, Children's Service Worker Case Manager, Children's Aid Society of the District of Thunder Bay
Katreena Scott, PhD, C.Psych., University of Toronto
Lisa Weldon, BSW, MSW, Family Service Worker, Children's Aid Society of Toronto
Keith Wilson, Child and Youth Counsellor, Madame Vanier Children's Services
Shannon Woolner, Substance Abuse Counsellor, Dave Smith Youth Treatment Centre

Preface

Aggression among young people is an important social issue. Young people who behave aggressively may harm not only themselves, but others. Moreover, children with serious aggression problems are more likely than children without such problems to become teenagers who have problems with aggression, with other mental health issues, or with substance use; and as adults they are more likely to engage in acts of violence. Fortunately, there is mounting evidence that early intervention and treatment for children who show signs of aggression can significantly reduce these harmful outcomes.

Many thousands of Canadians work or volunteer in a variety of settings with children and youth who have problems with anger and aggression. Teachers and school administrators, day-care and recreation centre workers, youth shelter workers, social service workers, sports coaches, youth leaders, camp counsellors and camp directors—all must be prepared to handle difficult behaviour at a moment's notice while ensuring the safety of all concerned. Their efforts, while fraught with challenges, are critical in addressing the emotional and behavioural problems that often impede the educational and social goals of young people.

Our understanding of the many contributing causes of aggression in children and youth has grown immensely over the past decade, and there are many evidence-based approaches available today to help those involved with young people who are showing problems. The information in this book is drawn from the research and experience of child psychologists, child psychiatrists, special education teachers, and mental health and substance use counsellors. The chapters are organized in a manner that presents and builds on developmental knowledge, then applies this knowledge to an understanding of and response to aggressive behaviour. We hope you find the material both inspiring and pertinent to your important work with children and youth.

David A. Wolfe, Editor

Introduction

You can make a difference

Isabella, age seven, doesn't like the drawing she has made of her house. She rips up her paper and throws the pieces at the girl seated in class beside her.

Eleven-year-olds Dylan and Jamal skate off the ice at the end of a peewee hockey game. Dylan gives Jamal a shove, blaming him for missing a goal and causing their team to lose.

Jealous of Sarah's midnight curfew, 14-year-old Maria turns on her friend, spreading rumours that Sarah is sleeping with another girl's boyfriend.

Sixteen-year-old James purposely brushes his hand across the breast of a schoolmate as she passes him in a crowded hallway.

If you work or volunteer with young people, you've probably seen situations similar to those mentioned on the previous page. Though the incidents are very different, all of them involve aggressive behaviour.

Do you know how to respond effectively when a young person behaves aggressively? Do you know what kinds of aggression are considered normal for a young person's age and stage of development? Do you know what kinds of aggression may suggest that a young person has a problem that needs specialized intervention?

The aim of this book is to help you answer "yes" to these questions. It describes the causes of aggressive behaviour in young people, and discusses approaches to handling it. Specifically, the book:
- explains various types of aggressive behaviour exhibited by young people
- identifies factors related to aggressive behaviour
- distinguishes between normal aggression and aggression that is of greater concern in young people
- gives practical advice on how to address aggression in children and youth
- highlights prevention and intervention strategies that have been proven through research to be effective, and indicates strategies that should be avoided
- discusses assessment and diagnoses for more serious aggressive behaviour exhibited by young people.

Interspersed throughout the book, you will find case studies that illustrate how treatments have benefited young people of various ages who have shown problems with aggression.

In the past, you may have found it hard to manage aggressive behaviour in a young person. You may have felt frustrated, impatient or angry, and may have raised your voice or spoken harsh words. This book will help you understand that young people who behave aggressively are not bad or deserving of blame. They need to know that you care about them and that you are willing to help them solve their problems. The earlier a child with aggression problems is identified and treated, the greater the chance that the chosen treatment will have lasting benefits.

A note on culture and aggression

Many of us, quite naturally, react to people and situations based on experiences and perspectives that are rooted in our own culture. Most of the information on aggression in this book is based on research rooted in western ideas and values. North American society, however, is becoming more and more culturally diverse. Experts recognize that family background, culture and religion can influence all types of behaviour—including aggression. What might be considered unusual or problematic behaviour in one culture may be seen as normal and acceptable in another.

Therefore, if you work or volunteer with young people, you will find it valuable to become more aware of your own attitudes and theirs. Ask yourself questions about what experiences from your past, in particular your cultural upbringing, have influenced you to develop certain views. Think about whose ideas have influenced your own, and where those ideas may have come from. Consider taking steps to learn about the cultures of the young people with whom you are involved.

A note on the language used in this book

Young people includes children (ages zero to 11) and youth (ages 12 to 18). We sometimes discuss these groups separately because the behaviours of each are different.

Parents includes parents, guardians, foster parents, group home workers or any other people (such as grandparents, aunts and uncles) who raise young people full time.

Caregivers includes nannies, babysitters and others who help parents look after their children.

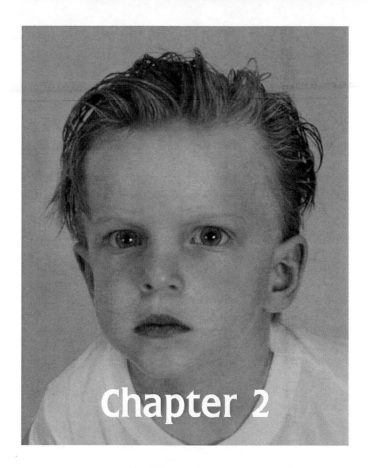

Chapter 2

About aggression

What is aggression?

Seventeen-year-old Carlos was angry at his classmate Zachary. During a recent math test, Zachary refused to allow Carlos to cheat from his paper. To get back at him, Carlos sent Zachary a cellphone text message with a death threat.

Fifteen-year-old Robert threw lighted matches into some dry leaves in the yard of his school until they caught fire. The fire spread and burned down an empty school portable.

Modern thinkers in different fields have wrestled with the topic of aggression. They have included pioneers in psychiatry, such as Sigmund Freud; experts who study animal behaviour, such as well-known observer of African chimpanzees Jane Goodall; and Albert Einstein, the famous scientist and promoter of world peace.

In struggling to understand aggression, experts have tried to define it at the outset of their work. What exactly is aggression? Biting, punching, kicking and other violent physical acts come immediately to mind, but the following definition reveals that other, less obvious, non-physical actions also constitute aggression.

> *Aggression is an action or threat of action that is intended to harm another person, either physically or psychologically.*

Types of aggression

Experts in various fields of study divide aggressive behaviour into a number of different categories:
• overt and covert aggression
• reactive and proactive aggression
• physical, verbal and social aggression
• sexual aggression (including dating violence)
• bullying.

Below you will find definitions and discussion of these different kinds of aggression, as well as some common examples. The categories can overlap— for example, sexual aggression can take both physical and verbal forms, and physical aggression can be either reactive or proactive. Thus, several of the terms listed above might apply to any one aggressive incident.

Some suggestions are given below about how to address the problem of young people engaging in particular types of aggression. Note, however, that not every suggestion will work for every young person or in every situation. You may have to try a variety of strategies until you find the one, or ones, that best fit your circumstances.

Overt aggression

Overt aggression refers to open, harmful acts directed at others; these acts may be physical or verbal *(see below)*. Overtly aggressive acts are performed in an obvious, even blatant way.

Covert aggression

Covert aggression refers to hidden activities intended to harm others. They can cause just as much damage as overtly aggressive acts, and can be more difficult to detect. Examples include lying, cheating, stealing and setting fires.

Reactive aggression

> *Three-year-old Amina enjoyed playing with the bowls of plastic fruit at her day care. When her playmate, Maria, tried to take a plastic banana away from her, Amina grabbed the toy back and bit Maria on the arm.*

Young people sometimes respond with aggression to frustration, teasing or threats. Experts call this type of behaviour *reactive aggression.* Young people who are impulsive, who act quickly without any thought, or who mistakenly believe that others feel hostile toward them are more likely than others to display reactive aggression. Young people also display different forms and degrees of reactive aggression depending upon their age and level of emotional development.

For example, toddlers (such as three-year-old Amina, described above) often react with physical aggression in response to frustration. Due to their lack of emotional maturity, they may bite, hit or push if they discover a playmate grabbing one of their toys. You can respond to such acts of reactive aggression in toddlers by slowly teaching them social skills. Here are a few ideas:

• Give the immediate, strong, and consistent message that aggression is not acceptable. For example: "No. Don't bite. Biting hurts." Repeat this message right away, in a calm, clear voice, each and every time the child bites.
• Let the toddler know, as quickly as possible, that aggression will not work. When Amina bites a child in order to get back her toy, she should not be allowed to keep it.
• Tell the toddler that he or she needs to learn to ask for permission to play with a toy, and that sharing with friends is fun. You can begin encouraging these social skills even before a child knows how to speak and is emotionally ready to share.
• Remove the toddler from a situation to give him or her a chance to calm down and understand your message. In a day care setting, for example, lead the child to a quiet place in the room. A short "time out" from a situation—even just a minute—works best for most toddlers. Disciplining toddlers too harshly leads to more, not less, aggression.
• Remember to praise toddlers when you see them sharing a favourite toy or showing kindness, empathy and affection toward other children. Even more than setting limits and consequences, the praising of exemplary social behaviours can encourage young people of all ages to act toward others in positive ways.

Proactive aggression

> During the winter months, a group of 10-year-old boys liked to
> throw snowballs at each other at recess. Manuel played more
> roughly than the other boys. He formed hard-packed, icy balls and
> whipped them at anyone he could. On occasion, he would ask Ravi
> to give him money. Manuel told Ravi that, if he gave him money, he
> wouldn't throw snowballs at him. Ravi often gave Manuel his
> allowance money.

Young people, like adults, sometimes deliberately choose to behave aggressively
with a goal in mind. Experts call this type of behaviour *proactive aggression.*

If you work with young people, you will want to consider a variety of options to
manage incidents of proactive aggression. Whatever action you decide to take
will depend upon a number of factors.

Consider the case involving Manuel and Ravi. One young person is gaining
power—and wealth—by means of aggressive behaviour. If you were a teacher
working at these boys' school, you could begin by arranging meetings to discuss
the incident, involving you, Manuel, Ravi, their parents and the principal. The
principal could tell Ravi that, if he's being threatened or bribed by another child,
he should tell his teacher or parents or another trusted adult. The adult would
then be able to help him solve his problem. The principal could also work with
Manuel's parents to set appropriate consequences if his behaviour persists. (Note
that some Canadian school boards, as part of Safe School programs, have set
rules and consequences to deter snowball throwing on school property.)

The proactive aggression case described above is also an example of bullying.
A section on bullying is included at the end of this chapter. It contains helpful
information about what you can do to help prevent and discourage bullying
behaviours. The material on bullying is also relevant to the following discussions
of physical, verbal and social aggression.

Physical aggression

This is the most widely recognized kind of aggression. From infancy through
adolescence, young people engage in a wide range of physically aggressive
behaviours. These can include poking and pinching, pushing and shoving,
knocking things out of someone's hands, tripping, hitting, kicking, throwing
things at others and even giving serious beatings leading to injury or, in rare
cases, death.

How common is physical aggression among young people? The National Longitudinal Survey of Children and Youth (NLSCY), a large Canadian study, provided a number of interesting findings on this question. The survey researchers defined aggression as "physical acts oriented towards another person which could inflict physical harm." (Very few studies have investigated the rate of verbal or social aggression.) They asked questions about whether the children in the study got into many fights; kicked, bit or hit other children; or reacted with anger and fighting when harmed accidentally by another child.

The survey results revealed the following statistics on physical aggression:
• Among children two years of age, 62 per cent of boys and 77 per cent of girls were classified, according to a set of criteria, as "low aggressive"; four per cent of boys and two per cent of girls were classified as "high aggressive."
• Among two- to four-year-olds, 3.5 per cent of children were classified as "high aggressive."
• Among five- to 11-year-olds, 3.3 per cent of boys and 0.6 per cent of girls were classified as "high aggressive."

Verbal aggression

"Sticks and stones will break my bones, but names can never hurt me." Young people have recited this old English saying for centuries. Though popular, and perhaps comforting, the saying is false: Names and cruel words can and do cause emotional harm. Children and youth can do significant damage to their peers by calling them names, insulting them or their families, and mocking or taunting them. Experts call this type of behaviour *verbal aggression.*

Boys and girls are equally likely to insult or taunt another person. Boys are more likely than girls to call others such names as "dumbo" or "asshole." Girls are more likely than boys to call others "slut" and "bitch." Adolescents may also tease and taunt by calling one another "gay" or other terms related to sexual orientation. *(You will find a discussion of this form of verbal aggression in the section on homophobic bullying on page 13.)*

If you work with young people, you can help to prevent and stop incidents of verbal aggression. Some younger children might be unaware that name calling is a form of aggression, so your first step might be to explain to them that verbal aggression can badly hurt another person, just like physical aggression can. Make it clear to the young people that, if they repeatedly use words to taunt others, they are bullying. *(See the section on bullying at the end of this chapter.)*

In a classroom, club, camp or shelter setting, consider asking young people to act out situations involving verbal aggression. Encourage children and youth not only to speak up about how they feel when they are taunted, but also to talk about how they feel when they are doing the taunting. If they say that taunting gives them the feeling that they are better than those around them, you can suggest other, more positive, ways of obtaining feelings of self-worth—for example, working to excel at school or at a sport.

Social aggression

> Ariana sat down in the school cafeteria to eat her lunch. She saw her friend Smita sitting with a group of girls. Smita whispered something to the other girls, and then they all looked over at Ariana and started to laugh.

Young people sometimes spread gossip or rumours, manipulate friendships or exclude one person from a group. Experts call this type of behaviour *social aggression.* Social aggression, which has recently become a focus of media attention, may occur more often among girls than boys. In any case, girls report having more negative feelings due to incidents involving social aggression.

If you work or volunteer with young people, there are a number of things you can do to tackle this challenging problem. Be sure that the strategies you employ are suited to the ages of the young people involved.

You may have to communicate to the young people you work with what behaviours constitute social aggression, because such behaviours are sometimes subtle and difficult to pin down. Young people may not recognize them as aggressive at all. In some North American studies, for example, preschool children have reported that they believe social aggression is less wrong and less likely to be punished than other forms of aggression. When working with young children, therefore, your best approach is to first tell them outright that social aggression is unacceptable and hurtful. If children perceive that adults view social aggression as wrong, they are less likely to use social aggression and more willing to seek adult help if, for example, someone is gossiping about them.

Some young people may display social aggression because they are angry at another person. They may be caught in an emotional struggle between feeling angry and a desire to be nice. One way to reduce social aggression, therefore, is to encourage young people to express their feelings more directly. It can also be helpful to stimulate discussions about conflict in relationships and how to deal with such conflicts in constructive ways.

Studies show that North American teenaged girls spend almost 20 per cent of their time talking to or being with friends. During this unstructured time, they have many opportunities to engage in social aggression. If you work with young people, you can encourage them to participate in structured activities (for example, clubs, sports, music programs, volunteer work) that will provide them with another outlet for their leisure time and enable them to feel part of a group.

Sexual aggression

Sexual acts (of any kind) performed without the voluntary agreement of the other person are defined as *sexual aggression.* Sexual aggression can include any behaviour from a kiss or a touch to rape. In Canada, the federal Criminal Code makes it illegal to commit sexually aggressive acts, which are classified under the broad heading of sexual assault. One form of sexual assault that has been the subject of much media attention in the past decade is date rape, in which non-consensual sex occurs between people who are in a romantic relationship.

Experts have identified the use of alcohol and other drugs as a contributing factor in sexual aggression among young people. When under the influence of some substances, young people are more likely to misinterpret friendly cues as sexual invitations and, conversely, are more at risk of losing the ability to assert their wishes or ward off a potential attack. Certain drugs, such as Rohypnol (flunitrazepan), are known as "date rape drugs" because they make sexual aggression easier to carry out. Rohypnol is a tranquillizer that can be slipped into a drink, producing sedative effects, loss of memory and unconsciousness.

Studies have shown that, among high school students, both boys and girls consider some non-consensual sexual activity to be OK under certain dating conditions—they don't think of the aggressive partner as engaging in sexual assault. Many teens also mistakenly think of rapists only as strangers, not realizing that acquaintances who are known to them can be rapists, too.

If you work or volunteer with adolescents, consider including in your program some discussion of sexual aggression and the steps that young people can take to prevent this problem. A good place to start is with the definitions of *sexual assault, rape* and *date rape.*

It can also be a good idea to discuss safety in dating. Here are some tips to share if you work with teens:
- Know where you are going. When you go out, make sure that someone (your brother or sister, a parent or a friend) knows where you will be. Know how to get home on your own, and have enough money on you to do so.
- Suggest going out on a group date if you feel uncomfortable going out as a couple.
- Plan to go to places where a lot of people are around.
- Don't use drugs (including alcohol) that can alter your thinking and your behaviour.
- Keep an eye on your drink—whether or not it's alcoholic—at all times.

- Know you have the right to say "no." Don't have sex just because someone else is paying for the date.
- Don't interpret a "no" as a "yes." If you are getting a double message from your partner, speak up and ask for a clarification of what he or she wants.
- Be aware that your size and physical presence might be intimidating.
- Remember that intoxication is not a legal defence. You are responsible for your actions, whether you are drunk or sober.
- Be aware that having sex is not necessarily tied to expressing or receiving love.
- If you don't want to do something, don't give in because someone asks you repeatedly, or because saying "yes" is easier to do than saying "no."

Dating violence

Experts define *dating violence* as an act of aggression, or the threat of such an act, by one member of an unmarried couple against the other member within the context of dating or courtship. Dating violence is, in many ways, similar to bullying. It involves a relationship between a more powerful person and a less powerful one, and it consists of repeated aggressive behaviour that can be physical, verbal, emotional or sexual in form.

If you work or volunteer with youth, consider integrating discussions about dating violence into your program or curriculum. You could, for example, encourage discussion about what kinds of behaviour the participants think are permissible and not permissible within the bounds of a relationship. Stress that healthy relationships are based on respect, not power.

Bullying

Bullying is harmful, repeated aggressive behaviour that can be physical, verbal or social in form. It involves a relationship between a more powerful person or group and a less powerful person or group. The power of a young person who bullies may come from being stronger, larger, older or more popular, or from having some sensitive information about the person being bullied.

Young people can be bullied over the differences, real or imagined, between them and the bullies. They might be bullied because they are new to a school, smaller than average, of a different culture or sexual orientation or from a less socially or economically advantaged family. They might lack social skills, or be shy, sensitive or annoying. In fact, they can be bullied for any reason—or for no reason at all.

Bullying can take place anywhere: on school grounds, on neighbourhood streets, in parks and recreation centres, at summer camps and in homes. Many incidents of bullying also involve other young people who are watching and not directly participating in the aggressive behaviour.

Homophobic bullying

> *Fourteen-year-old Habib was heading for the shower after his high-school football team's practice. He wrapped a towel around his waist and put on his flip-flops. Max, one of the biggest boys on the team, looked down at Habib's sandals. "You're so gay," he said in a loud voice, taunting Habib the same way he did at the end of every practice. As usual, the other boys started to laugh.*

Young people sometimes bully other young people by calling them names like "gay," "fag," "fairy," "queer," "lezzie" or "dyke." Experts call this all-too-common form of verbal aggression *homophobic bullying.*

Young people who experience homophobic bullying may or may not be gay. They may be straight but simply talk, behave or dress in a manner that is somehow different from that of the majority. They could be privately gay, openly gay or unsure of their sexual orientation.

Cyber-bullying

> *Students attending a private high school for boys in Toronto built a website filled with Nazi imagery and anti-Semitic slurs. When a student at a girls' school learned of the site and sent an e-mail message to a chat board asking that the site be taken offline, she received a stream of anti-Semitic messages in response to her protest.*

Digital technologies play a central role in youth culture. Today's teens can form virtual cliques by communicating through online chat rooms, bulletin boards and by e-mail. Instant messaging allows two young people, or a whole group, to talk together at the same time. Teens use their cellphones to send each other voice messages, text messages, digital photographs, even mini-movies.

These technologies provide young people with a new forum for socializing—and, unfortunately, for bullying. Cellphones, for example, can instantly send a text message containing a brief "hello"; they can just as instantly send a death threat. An adolescent girl can return home from school to find a photo of herself, standing half-dressed in her school's locker room, posted on a website.

How common is bullying?

Various studies have shown that when young people are together in groups, bullying happens often. In one Canadian study, 10 to 15 per cent of students in grades 5 to 10 reported being bullied. Videotaping a school setting showed that incidents involving bullying occurred about once every seven minutes on a playground and about once every 25 minutes in a classroom. A Canadian survey focusing on cyber-bullying found that 14 per cent of young Canadians had been threatened using instant messaging; 16 per cent admitted they had sent hateful comments.

The effects of bullying

The harmful effects of bullying should not be made light of or denied by adults. Young people who are bullied can:
• experience a loss of self-esteem and feelings of humiliation
• fear going to school
• become anxious or depressed.

Young people who are bullied, as well as those who bully, are more likely than those not involved with bullying behaviours to:
• feel lonely
• have trouble making friends
• fail at school
• become involved in delinquent and anti-social behaviours.

The two teenaged boys who shot and killed 12 students and a teacher at Columbine High School in Littleton, Colorado, in 1999 had been subject to homophobic bullying by their peers.

Cyber-bullying can be more troublesome than in-person bullying because young people can't get away from it. In the past, a child or youth who was being bullied at school could escape by going home. Furthermore, young people who use digital technologies to bully others may feel freer to make nastier comments than they would during face-to-face encounters. They might believe that they can't be identified and won't have to deal with any consequences.

Young people who bully are more likely than those who don't to develop into adults who continue to exert their power to harm others. As adults, they are more likely than average to engage in such aggressive behaviours as sexual harassment, dating violence, marital violence, child or elder abuse and workplace harassment, all of which have elements in common with bullying.

What you can do to discourage bullying

If you work or volunteer with young people in a school or other setting, you will likely need to confront the issue of bullying at some point. Consider creating a bullying prevention program; a good way to start is to form an anti-bullying committee with members representing different groups or stakeholders. For example, in a school setting, this committee could be made up of teachers, administrators, parents, caregivers and responsible students.

A good first task for this committee is to prepare an educational package that lays out what behaviours (physical, verbal or social) constitute bullying and makes clear that these behaviours are forms of aggression that harm others. Next, committee members could write a formal "Dignity for All" policy statement. Such a statement might declare, for example, that all young people, no matter their age, social background, culture, religion or spirituality, abilities, gender, sexual orientation or socio-economic situation, have an equal right to learn and participate in programs in a safe environment that is free of all forms of bullying. Finally, the committee can define a set of clear rules and procedures against bullying.

These rules and procedures should make it clear that young people who bully others will face specific consequences, and should outline what those consequences will be. They might include office detentions, meetings with parents, suspensions and, in extremely serious cases, police arrests. Consider including in the anti-bullying policy rules and procedures to deal with cyber-bullying, and specifying consequences even for behaviour that takes place off the school or organization's grounds. (The students who built the anti-Semitic website in Toronto mentioned above were expelled from their school as a result of their actions.)

Once a bullying prevention program has been put in place, the anti-bullying committee needs to make sure that all those who work at the organization are informed about it. This can be accomplished through meetings and written materials. In a school setting, teachers can use class time to discuss the subject of bullying, the "Dignity for All" policy statement and anti-bullying rules and procedures. Teachers, school administrators or members of the anti-bullying committee could also present details of the bullying prevention program at assemblies.

In one Canadian city, members of the local police force routinely visit school classrooms and give video presentations on bullying. They inform the students that, in some instances, bullying consists of assault or harassment, both of which are criminal behaviours.

Bullying prevention programs only work when schools set up a system of supervision, involving staff and responsible students, to make sure that the program's rules and procedures are consistently enforced. Some programs focus on positively engaging young people who may be watching incidents of bullying: convincing the children or youth who see a bullying incident not only to stop themselves from joining in, but to intervene on behalf of the person who is being bullied. Young people should also be encouraged to report to adults any incidents of bullying they encounter, whether or not they are the ones being bullied.

It's useful for bullying prevention programs to also include discussions about the responsible and ethical use of the Internet. Young people should be informed, for example, that online bullying can be illegal: under the Criminal Code of Canada, it's a crime to communicate repeatedly with someone if your communication causes them to fear for their own safety or the safety of others. It's also a crime to post something on a website that is designed to insult a person or likely to injure a person's reputation by exposing him or her to hatred, contempt or ridicule. Young people should also be cautioned that cyberspace is not anonymous. In fact, every time they access the Internet, a traceable Internet Protocol address or electronic fingerprint is created.

Better informed young people will make better decisions about their social use of the Internet. Consider asking the young people in your organization to write online contracts that outline the ways in which they will and will not use digital technologies.

In the end, it is not visits by the police that will prevent bullying among young people, but a culture based on peacefulness, nurturing and caring. Children and youth need to develop their own moral code so they will consciously choose to behave ethically.

The ideas mentioned above form the core of a successful bullying prevention program. There are also other things your organization can do to help prevent bullying. You might suggest, for example, that your school's curriculum be adapted to include human relations education. This kind of education program fosters an appreciation of people of different social, cultural and religious backgrounds, and of different sexual orientations. Other supportive educational programs teach social, conflict-resolution and decision-making skills *(see Chapter 7).*

Parents and caregivers can also play an important role in preventing bullying, particularly by:
• discussing the subject openly at home
• modelling and praising respectful and empathetic behaviour toward others
• providing adequate supervision
• responding responsibly to any known incidents of bullying with fair consequences.

Families can also work together to establish their own "Dignity for All" policies. Schools can help parents and others in their communities by distributing up-to-date information about bullying and prevention strategies. Parents and others can also lobby local school board representatives and politicians to establish city- or town-wide bullying prevention programs.

Creating an effective bullying prevention program takes planning and effort, but the payoff is significant. Results can include:
• fewer incidents of bullying and harassment
• fewer conflicts
• less gang activity
• better school attendance
• increased student attachment to the school.

One well-known program geared to young people aged six to 15, called the Olweus Bullying Prevention Program, was developed in Norway. Studies showed that this program reduced bullying problems by between 33 and 64 per cent for various subgroups. In addition, schools that adopted the program experienced lower rates of other conduct problems, such as theft, vandalism and truancy.

Chapter 3

Understanding aggression

Risk factors and protective factors

Seven-year-old Shana often pushed or hit other children in her class. She was verbally aggressive with adults, even when they approached her with kindness. She told her Grade 2 teacher that her clothing was ugly and that she had bad breath. When Shana's mother asked her to come to the dinner table or get ready for bed, Shana frequently scratched her.

What caused Shana to behave this way? The causes of human aggression are complex; there likely isn't a simple reason to explain why a child behaves aggressively. Similarly, there likely isn't a simple single way to manage or treat the child's aggressive behaviour.

Psychologists speak about *risk factors* and *protective factors* for aggressive behaviour. These are characteristics of individuals, their families and their environments that either increase (risk factors) or decrease (protective factors) the likelihood that the individuals will display aggressive behaviour.

Studies indicate that the more risk factors that are present in a young person's life, the greater the probability that he or she will develop problems with aggression. Risk factors are not a definite predictor, however. Young people with many risk factors will not necessarily be aggressive (perhaps because of counterbalancing protective factors in their lives), whereas young people with few risk factors can show a range of aggression problems.

Experts have used risk and protective factors not only as a model—a way of understanding the roots of aggressive behaviour—but also as a tool for developing and carrying out interventions or treatments for aggressive behaviour. *(For a discussion of these interventions, see Chapter 7.)*

Risk and protective factors are grouped into three broad categories:
• individual factors
• family factors
• environmental factors.

An understanding of these factors can help determine when a young person has a problem with aggression that requires more specialized intervention. The remainder of this chapter discusses the major factors related to aggression in children and youth within these categories.

Individual risk and protective factors

Temperament

Temperament refers to both inborn and acquired characteristics that influence how people relate to others and respond to situations. Studies have shown that young people with difficult temperaments are more likely to behave aggressively than those with more easygoing temperaments.

Children or youth who show one or more of the traits listed here tend to possess a difficult temperament; as well, young people with any or all of these traits tend to behave more aggressively than those who do not have them:
• difficulty adapting to new situations
• irritability or fussiness
• reluctance to smile or laugh
• tendency toward overactivity
• short attention span; difficulty focusing or completing a task

- irregular sleeping and eating habits
- tendency to engage in dangerous or potentially dangerous activities, seemingly without fear.

Children's temperaments are generally apparent by age three. However, some of these traits—such as fussiness, irritability, problems adapting to new situations, and rarely smiling or laughing—can emerge by the time an infant is six months old.

Emotional control

Young people differ in their ability to control the strength and expression of their moods, feelings and impulses. Those who have less emotional control tend to act more aggressively than those with more emotional control. Those with less emotional control are also more likely than average to show aggression and related behavioural problems throughout their adolescence and adulthood.

Young people with less emotional control tend to:
- show a low tolerance for frustration
- have difficulty controlling their tempers
- overreact to people and situations
- hold grudges for longer than average
- act impulsively.

Through the help of some types of therapy, especially cognitive-behavioural therapy, young people can learn to better understand and control their moods, feelings and impulses. They can also learn techniques for controlling specific emotions, such as anger, through specialized training programs. *(For information on helping to build young people's emotional control, see Chapter 7.)*

Social skills

Some young people lack important social skills, such as knowing how to behave and communicate in socially acceptable ways and to understand the feelings of others. These skills are necessary for developing positive relations with peers and adults. (The fact that toddlers are not emotionally developed enough to have acquired social skills accounts for the fact that rates of physical aggression are higher among them than among adolescents.) Young people of any age who lack social skills tend to behave more aggressively than those who have good social skills.

The ability to read *social signals*—to understand the subtle meaning implied by the behaviour of those around us—is a particularly important skill. Some young people are quick to assume that others around them are hostile or unfriendly. They may sense ill will in situations where none exists and in which they have been given no clear signals. They may, for example, see a student passing a note in class and immediately presume that the note says negative things about them. Misreading social signals in this way is a risk factor for aggression.

Young people can work to develop better social skills. *(For information on social skills training, see Chapter 7.)*

Empathy

Empathy is the ability to appreciate another person's situation, feelings and motives. It is a protective factor against aggression: young people who feel empathy for those around them are less likely to behave aggressively than those who are not empathetic.

Social skills training can sometimes help young people understand others' points of view and thus encourage the development of empathy *(see Chapter 7)*.

Self-concept

A young person's self-concept can be another protective factor against aggression. For example, a child or youth who has a strong cultural identity and is optimistic is less likely to behave aggressively than one who has a weak cultural identity and is pessimistic. High self-esteem has also been shown in studies to be a protective factor for aggression. Note, however, that some young people who behave aggressively do possess high self-esteem, but are grandiose and lack empathy for others.

If you work with young people who you think might be having problems due to feelings of low self-esteem, there are ways you can intervene. You could, for example, contact the person's parents to suggest that they look for a therapist who can counsel their child. Sometimes a young person's self-esteem is affected by family dynamics, in which case the whole family might benefit from counselling. Relationships with peers, teachers and others can also play significant roles. *(For more information about therapy, including family therapy, see Chapter 7.)*

IQ and success at school

IQ (intelligence quotient) is another factor that can influence the likelihood that young people will behave aggressively. Those who have lower-than-average IQs are slightly more likely than average to behave aggressively, while those who have higher-than-average IQs are less likely to behave aggressively. Thus, with respect to aggression, a low IQ is a small risk factor, and a high IQ is a protective factor.

One reason for this connection is that a high IQ can reflect a strong ability to use language—an ability that can enable young people to solve conflicts without resorting to aggression. (Note: Some people consider standard IQ tests to be culturally biased because they measure knowledge and skill sets that are specific to western culture. Thus, IQ tests may not accurately show the abilities of young people from other cultures.)

Young people who are successful at school (whether or not they have scored high on IQ tests) tend to behave less aggressively than those who are not successful: being successful at school is a protective factor against aggression.

If you believe that young people with whom you are working or volunteering have learning problems that are interfering with their school performance, you should take action as soon as possible to ensure that they get the extra help they need to fulfil their potential. Begin by contacting the parents—see if they will agree to assessments of their children, in order to determine if they have specific learning problems. *(For more information about assessments, see Chapter 6.)*

A variety of programs are available to help young people who have learning, reading, speaking or other difficulties. Programs are offered by some Canadian schools, mental heath organizations, social service agencies and private companies. Some schools can arrange for young people to have psychoeducational assistants help them in class. (Note: Enrolling a young person in a school-based special education program in Ontario requires that the school principal request an Identification, Placement and Review Committee [IPRC] meeting. At that meeting, the young person's case will be discussed to see if he or she qualifies to receive special education support.)

The sooner that young people with learning difficulties receive the help they need, the more likely they are to achieve success at school.

Hormones and neurotransmitters

Hormones and neurotransmitters can affect various forms of behaviour, including aggression.

Testosterone is a hormone produced in the testes of men and in the ovaries of women. The outer layer of the adrenal gland near the kidneys of both sexes also secretes testosterone. Research has shown an association between higher-than-average levels of circulating testosterone and aggressive behaviour in both men and women. It is still unknown, however, if higher-than-average testosterone levels are a cause of aggressive behaviour or merely an after-effect.

Serotonin is an organic compound found in animal and human tissue, especially in the brain, blood serum and gastric mucous membranes. It performs a number of functions in the body, including acting as a *neurotransmitter* (a compound that transmits information across the synapse, or gap, that separates one nerve cell from another nerve cell or a muscle). Some research has indicated a positive association between lower-than-average levels of serotonin and aggressive behaviour.

Substance use

Substance use—the use of alcohol and other drugs—is a risk factor for aggression among young people. *(For a full discussion of the complicated relationship between substance use and aggression, as well as how to reduce the harms caused by substance use, see the section on substance use disorders in Chapter 8.)*

Mental health disorders

Young people with certain mental health disorders tend to behave more aggressively than other people. The following disorders are risk factors for aggression:
• conduct disorder (CD)
• oppositional defiant disorder (ODD)
• attention-deficit/hyperactivity disorder (ADHD)
• some mood or psychotic disorders
• posttraumatic stress disorder (PTSD)
• substance use disorders (SUDs)
• fetal alcohol spectrum disorder (FASD).

(For a detailed discussion of these disorders and their relation to aggression, see Chapter 8.)

Family risk and protective factors

We learn a great deal about how to behave and how to react to the world from how our parents cared for us. And the ways in which our parents raised us were, in turn, influenced by the ways in which their parents raised them. Studies have shown that aspects of a young person's family life can act as either risk or protective factors with respect to aggression. Some of these aspects are discussed next.

Attachment

Attachment refers to the relationship of trust that forms between infants and parents or caregivers, whereby infants feel confident that the people who look after them will satisfy their needs and keep them safe. Parents or caregivers build the foundation for a secure attachment by responding sensitively to infants' needs and signs of distress—for example, picking up crying infants and trying to soothe them by offering them food, a change of diaper, an extra blanket or a cuddle. Perhaps contrary to what might be expected, infants who are soothed by their parents or caregivers tend to develop the ability to soothe themselves more easily than those whose signs of need and distress are not met with a caring response. And, as they get older, children who were soothed as infants are less likely to react aggressively under stress, because of this stronger ability to comfort themselves.

A secure attachment to a parent or caregiver during the first year of life also gives children a solid foundation for the development of trust, self-esteem, self-control, confidence and the ability to form healthy relationships with others. These qualities are protective factors that decrease the likelihood of children becoming aggressive.

Parents and caregivers can hinder the development of a secure attachment by not responding to infants' cries or other signs of need or distress. Children with an insecure attachment tend to avoid, be ambivalent about or actively resist their parents or caregivers. Studies show, too, that children who have been neglected and have an insecure attachment also have an increased risk of developing aggression.

Parents and caregivers may benefit from baby-care classes where they can learn skills that promote the development of a secure attachment with their infants. Such classes are offered at some hospitals, community health centres and other institutions.

Public health nurses in some Canadian cities also make home visits to help teach the skills necessary for good baby care. Numerous books on the subject are available at libraries and bookstores.

Discipline

Firm, fair and consistent discipline will best help a young person to develop appropriate social behaviours. It can also serve as a protective factor against aggression.

Inappropriate discipline consists of methods that are too harsh, too lenient or inconsistent. An old saying advises, "Spare the rod and spoil the child." Modern research, however, does not support this statement. Harsh discipline, particularly if it is physical, increases the risk that the child or youth who receives it will be aggressive. Young people who are hit while being disciplined are more likely to physically abuse others than are those who are not hit. Also, parents who hit may seriously injure their children.

Discipline that is too lenient is also a risk factor for aggression: children who are allowed to act inappropriately or anti-socially without facing any negative consequences are more likely to behave aggressively than those who are disciplined appropriately. Young people who never know what type of discipline to expect, or when to expect it (inconsistent discipline), are also at risk for aggressive behaviour.

If you know parents who would like to learn about better ways to discipline their children, you can suggest they take parent management skills training programs. *(For information on this subject, see Chapter 7.)*

Level of supervision

Lack of appropriate supervision is a key risk factor for aggression. Young people who are unsupervised are more likely than those who are well supervised to behave aggressively. Unsupervised children and youth simply have more opportunities to act in socially unacceptable ways without having to face consequences, and more opportunities to spend time with peers who act in unacceptable ways and may influence them to do the same.

An appropriate level of parental supervision is a protective factor against aggression. Parents can help reduce the likelihood that their children will display a range of behavioural problems by monitoring their children's activities consistently to ensure that they are spending their free time in positive ways. Consistent monitoring means that parents know where their children are, who they are with and what they are doing.

Adults other than parents are responsible for supervising young people as well. Appropriate supervision is as essential in school classrooms, hallways, washrooms, schoolyards and other community spaces as it is in the home. In fact, children often benefit from taking part in organized activities and youth groups where adults are present to supervise, guide and teach them.

Many community centres and religious institutions offer organized activities in which children and youth can take part for little or no cost. You can encourage parents to help their children enrol in them. And if you know parents who would like to learn how to supervise their children's time appropriately, you can suggest they take parent management skills training programs. *(For more information on such programs, see Chapter 7.)*

Family interaction

The ways in which parents act and interact with their children can be risk factors or protective factors with respect to aggression. Positive parental involvement is a key protective factor for aggression, especially during a young person's teen years.

Children who are raised by parents who reject them, who are cold and unsupportive, who don't communicate with them and who don't work through problems with them are at risk for behaving aggressively. Children who are raised by parents who use aggression to solve their own problems are also at risk.

On the other hand, children who are raised by parents who embrace them; who show them warmth and support, talk to them frequently and ask them questions about their thoughts, feelings and activities; who show them that they are ready to work through problems together; and who communicate positive expectations; are less likely to display aggression than those raised by non-nurturing parents.

Parents can also help to protect their children from developing aggressive behaviours by simply spending time with them doing leisure activities—such as playing games their children enjoy, reading to them or going skating together. The more time parents spend in positive ways with their children, the less likely their children are to behave aggressively.

Some families may benefit from family therapy, which is therapy that focuses on changing the way families interact. Its aim is to increase understanding and improve communication among family members, and it can help them spend positive time together. *(For more information on family therapy, see Chapter 7.)*

Family peace and stability

Family stability is a protective factor against aggression. The more stable their family environment, the smaller the likelihood that young people will behave aggressively. Conversely, the less stable their family environment, the greater the likelihood that young people will behave aggressively. Family instability can arise from marital conflicts, domestic violence, financial problems, frequent moves, or separation or divorce.

Unstable families may benefit in many ways from family therapy. *(See the section on family therapy in Chapter 7.)*

Child abuse and neglect

Neglect or abuse—physical, sexual or emotional—can have serious effects on the lifelong development of children and youth, and can lead to aggression and other anti-social behaviours.

Physical abuse refers to deliberate acts committed against a child by a parent or caregiver that cause injury, ranging from minor (such as bruising) to serious (such as broken bones or burns). *Sexual abuse* refers to any unwanted sexual act committed by one person against another, including kissing, fondling or intercourse. *Emotional abuse* refers to a variety of behaviours, including rejection, threats, humiliation, terrorizing, extremely harsh or erratic discipline, unrealistic expectations or excessive criticism. (Some experts feel that physical and sexual abuse always involve emotional abuse as well.) *Neglect* is defined as the failure to provide adequate food, clothing and shelter for, or appropriate supervision or medical care of, dependent children.

Young people who are abused or neglected are slightly more likely than average to behave aggressively. They are also at greater risk of developing other long-term emotional, health or behavioural problems. Abuse is more likely to occur in families facing many stresses than in those facing few stresses.

Child abuse and neglect are against Canadian law. If you are in contact with a young person whom you suspect might be experiencing abuse or neglect, contact an appropriate authority, such as the local Children's Aid Society. Some agencies offer effective child abuse prevention programs targeted to parents.

Parental traits, conditions or behaviours

Certain traits, conditions or behaviours of their parents put young people at risk for aggression. Young people whose parents behave anti-socially or criminally are more likely to behave aggressively than those raised by parents who are socially well adjusted and law abiding. Young people whose parents have substance use problems are also more likely to behave aggressively than those whose parents do not have those problems.

The reasons why the traits, conditions or behaviours of parents put their children at risk for aggression are complex. One aspect is that parents can negatively influence young people by modelling—and thus indirectly teaching them— inappropriate behaviours. In addition, substance use and other problems can negatively affect parents' caregiving style, sometimes to the point of child abuse or neglect.

Being born to a mother who experiences depression is also a risk factor for aggression. Depression can affect a mother's ability to respond appropriately to her baby's needs and prevent her from feeling warmth for her children.

A number of treatment programs to help young people who have aggression problems are designed to reduce the behavioural, substance use and mental health problems of their parents or guardians. *(For more information on these programs, see Chapter 7.)*

Teen motherhood

Children born to teenaged mothers are much more likely to behave aggressively than children born to adult mothers. The reasons for this are complicated. Parents still in their teens may not have the knowledge or funds they need to properly care for their children. They are more likely than older mothers to have dropped out of school and to have lower-than-average incomes. They are also more likely to have had children with fathers who behave anti-socially, or to spend time with men who act in anti-social ways.

Teenaged mothers are more likely than older mothers to be raising their children alone, without financial and emotional support. This lack of support can increase the stress of parenting, which, in turn, can have a negative impact on the mothers' parenting styles. The risk of aggression is highest among young people born to teenaged mothers who are isolated and poorly educated and have lower-than-average incomes.

A number of effective programs are available both for young people who have aggression problems and for teenaged mothers. These programs address, as part of treatment, the problems that the mothers may be experiencing, such as marital problems, depression, and social and financial problems. *(For more information on treatment programs, see Chapter 7.)*

SHANA'S STORY
Risk and protective factors

At the outset of this chapter, we met seven-year-old Shana, who pushed and hit other children in her class and was verbally abusive to her teachers. Shana also often refused to comply with her mother's requests and frequently scratched her.

Upon the advice of her teacher, Shana's mother, Charmaine, took her daughter to a child psychiatrist. As the psychiatrist got to know Shana, she discovered a range of risk and protective factors with respect to aggression. She discovered, for example, that Shana had been born to a teenaged mother who was not caring for her properly (a risk factor for aggression). Shana's mother was poorly educated, worked as a prostitute, had a substance use problem and had no family support network. When working with Shana, the psychiatrist discovered that Shana was intelligent (a protective factor for aggression) but had poor communication and other social skills. She also had a mental health problem called *oppositional defiant disorder (see Chapter 8).*

In developing a treatment plan for Shana's aggressive behaviour, the psychiatrist tried to reduce the influences of risk factors in Shana's life. *(Shana's treatment plan is outlined in Chapter 7.)*

Environmental risk and protective factors

Economic and social family living conditions

Young people from families living in conditions that are economically or socially disadvantaged are more likely, if other risk factors exist, to behave aggressively than those from families living in conditions that are economically and socially advantaged.

There are many reasons why the likelihood of aggression among young people can be connected to their families' living conditions. Families with lower incomes may, for example, not have enough money to consistently fulfil their children's physical and social needs. While some families with lower incomes may have enough money to pay for food and accommodation, they may not have funds left over to pay for extracurricular activities. Participating in such activities can be a protective factor against the development of aggressive behaviour *(see "Extracurricular activities" later in this chapter.)* Families with lower incomes may also be forced to live in unsafe neighbourhoods, which is a risk factor *(see below)*. Financial worries can also be stressful for parents, and the stress caused by such worries can reduce their ability to provide proper discipline and supervision, and a positive family environment for their children.

(Chapter 7 presents ideas on how we can work together to improve families' social and economic living conditions.)

Neighbourhood

Living in a socially advantaged neighbourhood is a protective factor against aggression in young people.

Living in an unsafe neighbourhood—one marked by the presence of gangs, drug dealing and other criminal activities—is a risk factor for aggression. Young people who grow up in unsafe neighbourhoods are exposed to more violence than those who grow up in safe neighbourhoods. They see it, hear about it, experience it and fear it. Some may become desensitized to violence. Others may develop symptoms of posttraumatic stress disorder (PTSD), which is linked to aggression problems *(for a discussion of PTSD, see Chapter 8)*. Young people who live in unsafe neighbourhoods are more likely to come into contact with peers who behave in socially unacceptable ways, and to be negatively influenced by them. They are also more likely to join gangs.

Urban neighbourhoods form distinct "villages," each with its own character. Residents of unsafe neighbourhoods tend to have little education and low incomes, and to lack social power and a sense of community attachment. It takes energy, collective will and social and political activism to try to change the character of an unsafe neighbourhood. *(Chapter 7 presents ways in which people can work together to bring about this kind of change.)*

School

Attending a poorly run or unsafe school is another risk factor for aggression among young people, while attending a well-run and safe school is a protective factor.

Poorly run schools are those with inadequate monitoring and supervision of students, unfair and inconsistent discipline, behavioural rules and expectations that are not clear, and no consequences for students who break the rules. Such schools mirror poorly functioning families. Students in unsafe schools are exposed to bullying, harassment and other forms of violence.

Poorly run and unsafe schools do not foster good morale or a sense of attachment among students and teachers. Students who do not feel attached to their schools do not succeed as well academically; they tend to skip classes and drop out more often than students who feel attached to their schools.

Conversely, being successful at school is a protective factor for young people. Students who attend well-run, safe schools are more likely to feel attached to their school, to succeed academically and to avoid aggressive behaviour.

One way to help create a safe, well-run school that fosters attachment among students and staff is to implement an anti-bullying program. *(Suggestions for doing this are given in the section on bullying in Chapter 2.)*

Peer influence

The relationships young people have with their peers can affect their likelihood of behaving aggressively. Younger children, for example, may shy away from playing with peers who behave aggressively. Therefore, those who behave aggressively sometimes attract only friends who also behave aggressively— or, sometimes, no friends at all. Young children without friends miss out on key opportunities to develop good personal and social skills, both of which are protective factors against aggression.

Peer influence is even more powerful during adolescence. The pressure of their peers can either reduce or increase the probability that young people will behave aggressively. Teens with friends who behave aggressively are more likely than others to accept aggressive behaviour and to behave aggressively themselves. Teens with friends who have other conduct problems—for example, problems involving substance use and rule breaking—are more likely to have conduct problems themselves than are teens whose friends do not have such problems.

As well, teens who lack close relationships with their parents are particularly likely to be negatively influenced by peers.

Managing negative peer influences among teens can be challenging, because teens can choose to distance themselves from their families or other supportive adults. Mentoring programs have been shown to help some teens who lack positive parental involvement *(see Chapter 7)*.

Gangs

Gang association is another risk factor for aggression.

A *youth gang* is a group of youth who interact at a high rate among themselves to the exclusion of others. A gang often has a name and claims a geographical area of influence and activity. Youth gangs engage in criminal behaviour of varying seriousness.

Young people join gangs for many reasons. Some may feel a need to belong to peer groups or substitute families, especially if their own families do not function well. Some may be seeking feelings of pride—in their culture, their language or their neighbourhood. Others may join gangs because they want money and power, or an outlet for hostility in an arena where crime and fighting are praised. Still others join because they need someone to lead them.

Young people who are involved with gangs are more likely than those who are not to show, to have experienced or to have been exposed to the following:
• aggressive, anti-social behaviour
• impulsiveness
• negative role models
• harsh, punitive discipline
• difficulty with structured school
• streetwise behaviour
• truancy from school
• an arrest before age 14
• connections to a delinquent or violent peer group
• a pattern of criminal activity in the family
• a pattern of violence in the family
• drug use
• drug trafficking
• access to firearms
• norms that support violence as a means to an end.

Gang-involved youth commit more violent and criminal acts (especially drug dealing) than youth who stay away from gangs. In joining a gang, young people may be influenced by what psychologists call a *pack mentality*, in which individuals react together as one group rather than following their own instincts or consciences.

Sometimes groups of youths that are perceived as gangs by other community members are in fact simply friendship groups. Their members often behave in ways that are similar to the ways gang members behave: forming exclusive social relationships, wearing a similar style of dress and claiming a popular "hangout spot" as their turf. But such friendship groups do not take part in violent or criminal activity.

Community-based interventions are needed to help reduce the presence of gangs in neighbourhoods. *(For more information on such interventions, see Chapter 7.)*

Media

Experts have conducted a great deal of research on how the media—particularly violent television shows—influence aggression. This research has shown that young people in general become more aggressive after watching violent shows, and that those with pre-existing aggressive tendencies tend to become even more aggressive.

Interestingly, it is not just violence on TV but TV itself that appears to affect young people's levels of aggression. A study of school-aged children showed that children who watched more TV, whether the programs were violent or not, reported more aggressive behaviour than those who watched less. As the number of TV hours per day increased, so did the number of reported violent behaviours. Young people who watch a lot of television may become desensitized to real-life violence. They may also come to the pessimistic belief that the world is a dangerous place.

Playing video games may have similar effects on young people to those of watching TV, but further research is needed before conclusions can be drawn.

Because of the prevalence of television programs and video games, it's difficult for parents to ban their children from watching or playing them. However, parents can set clear limits on the amount of time their children engage in these activities. Moreover, parents can discourage young people from watching shows and playing games that promote anti-social behaviours, are violent or glorify violence as a way of dealing with conflicts.

Young people can also be encouraged to spend their leisure time doing other activities instead of watching TV, such as working on hobbies, art, sports or chores *(see the next page for suggestions on involving young people in extracurricular activities)*.

Extracurricular activities

Participation in extracurricular activities is a protective factor against aggression in young people. Examples of extracurricular activities include art classes, music lessons, volunteer work and sports (team or individual). These activities give young people opportunities to build self-esteem, release stress and develop positive personal and social skills. They also consume leisure hours, leaving less unsupervised time in which to engage in aggressive and other anti-social behaviours.

The participation of their parents in a hobby or other leisure activity of their own is also a protective factor for aggression among children. Participating in activities outside the home or workplace can give parents a chance to find release from their daily stresses, which can increase their patience—as well as their mental and emotional energy for providing a positive family environment.

Mentors

A solid relationship with at least one caring adult who supports, approves of and respects a young person can be a protective factor for aggression. The mentoring adult in a young person's life might be a parent, an extended family member (such as a grandparent, aunt or uncle) or a teacher. Young people's relationships with their mentors can add to, or even replace, their parents' support.

Mentoring programs (such as Big Brothers and Big Sisters) can help young people build solid relationships with caring adults. *(For more information, see Chapter 7.)*

Attachment to community

Feeling a sense of attachment to one's community can serve as a protective factor against aggression among young people. This attachment can be fostered in children and youth in a variety of ways—for example, through religious or cultural instruction, or through participation on school teams, in school clubs, or in community organizations.

KATYA'S STORY
Risk and protective factors

Katya moved to Canada from Russia when she was 16. At the time, she was a strong-willed and highly defiant teen who was often rude to her parents and teachers. She smoked a lot of marijuana and drank a lot of alcohol. Though rebellious, Katya was also intelligent, an excellent student and a gifted violinist.

As newcomers to Canada without many savings, Katya's family settled into an unsafe urban neighbourhood. Her father tried to start a business, while her mother worked as a homemaker. Focusing on coping with living in a new country, Katya's parents paid little attention to her.

A few months after the family's arrival in Canada, Katya was raped by neighbourhood gang members. They threatened her at gunpoint, saying they would kill her if she told anyone, and warned her that the only way to stay safe was to join the gang and pay the leader $300 each month for protection. Terrified, Katya became a gang member. She got into fights, beat up others and witnessed murders. In addition to smoking and drinking, she started using amphetamines heavily. She developed anxiety and eating disorders. Still, she managed to maintain high marks in school.

Katya's parents sought help for her problems from mental health care providers. As her counsellors got to know her, they worked with her to reduce the risk factors and strengthen the protective factors in her life.

What were Katya's risk factors? A difficult temperament, moving to a new country, substance use problems, living in an unsafe neighbourhood, having parents who paid little attention to her, experiencing sexual assault, gang membership and, possibly, posttraumatic stress disorder.

What were Katya's protective factors? High intelligence, confidence in her academic and musical abilities, a creative hobby, a resourceful nature and a relatively stable family life.

"Normal" aggression

As children grow up, they pass through a number of stages in which certain negative behaviours, including those involving aggression, are commonplace or "normal"—even expected. It is not unusual, for example, for a two-year-old girl to hit another child to get a favourite toy, or to have a temper tantrum if she doesn't get her way.

If you work with young people, you have probably seen many situations involving aggression. In the next section you will find an overview of the kinds of aggressive behaviours that most commonly occur during specific phases of development. *(Some kinds of normal aggression have already been discussed in Chapter 2, along with strategies for managing them.)* Gaining an understanding of what aggressive behaviours are normal in young people is a good first step in determining whether a young person has a problem with aggression that needs specialized intervention.

What is "normal" aggression?

Infants and toddlers (ages 0–2)

Experts do not consider any of the behaviours displayed by infants (children under a year old) to be aggressive. Aggression consists of an action or threat of action that is intended to harm another person, either physically or psychologically. Infants have not yet developed the level of awareness that would allow them to purposely harm another being. What they do exhibit, in particular from the ages of two to seven months, is an instinctive emotional response to being frustrated.

By the age of 12 to 18 months, however, children do begin to behave aggressively. In fact, almost half of social interactions between toddlers involve a conflict or disruption. The conflicts are physical, involving pushing, biting or hitting, and often arise from disputes over toys or attention. Conflicts such as these continue to be common among children until they are well over the age of two. As toddlers, boys and girls are equally likely to behave aggressively.

Two-year-olds are often aggressive when they're fighting over toys, or if others invade their space. They may commonly push, hit or bite. Their conflicts, however, tend to be brief.

(For more information about toddlers and aggression, see the discussion of reactive aggression in Chapter 2.)

Preschoolers (ages 3–5)

Between the ages of three and five, most children gradually learn to control their emotions. Perhaps as a result of this control, the frequency of physically aggressive behaviours slowly drops among preschool children, particularly around age four. Among siblings in this age group, however, almost half of all interactions still result in some type of conflict, which often erupts into physically aggressive behaviour.

While older preschoolers are less likely than younger ones to display physical aggression, as their language skills develop they begin to use verbal aggression. *(For more information about verbal aggression, see Chapter 2.)*

Among older preschoolers, differences begin to appear between boys and girls with respect to aggression. After the age of four, girls tend to be less physically aggressive than boys; they are more likely to smooth over conflicts with others. They are also more likely to manage or hide negative emotions and to follow social conventions. Young girls, however, are more likely than boys to use social aggression. A girl as young as three, in fact, may start to manipulate relationships—for example, telling another girl that she is not her friend anymore and that she will not invite her to her next birthday party. *(For more information about social aggression, see Chapter 2.)*

The reasons why differences between the genders exist with respect to aggression are complex. Some factors are connected to hormonal differences between girls and boys. Others are related to the different ways in which boys and girls are raised. Parents and caregivers of children in many cultures often send boys and girls a different set of messages about how they should behave: Girls are more likely than boys to be encouraged to avoid physical fights, to seek alternatives and to talk about their emotions. Boys, on the other hand, are more likely than girls to be allowed to openly express their anger and aggression; however, they are more likely to be encouraged to hide other emotions, particularly those showing vulnerability, such as sadness, fear or hurt.

School-aged children (ages 6–11)

Incidents involving physical aggression occur less often, and are less intense, among school-aged children than among those who are younger. Teasing, name calling and other types of verbal aggression, however, increase during these years, and occur equally often among boys and girls. During this stage of development, children also begin to bully each other. *(For a discussion of bullying, see the section on this topic in Chapter 2.)*

While the number and intensity of incidents involving physical aggression decline among children of both genders when they reach school age, boys continue to display more physical aggression than girls. Boys are more likely to fight, to bully others physically and to take part in rough-and-tumble play; they tend to be more direct, more confrontational and louder in their encounters than girls; and they are more likely than girls to assume that others have hostile intentions toward them. Boys are five times more likely than girls to have conduct problems.

While school-aged girls are less likely than boys in the same age group to show physical aggression, they commonly respond to certain situations with social aggression. For example, a third of all school-aged girls will, at times, spread rumours or try to manipulate friendships. *(For more information on social aggression, see Chapter 2.)*

Children of both genders in this age group are likely to behave differently at home than they do at school or in other social situations. Siblings, for example, are more likely to display physical aggression against each other than against non-family members.

Adolescents (age 12 and older)

Conflicts involving physical aggression occur less often among teenagers than among younger school-aged children. Less than five per cent of teenaged boys use physical aggression, and an even smaller percentage of teenaged girls do so. (Teenaged girls tend to deal with conflicts using negotiation and compromise in order to protect their relationships. They also tend to become submissive or withdraw from a conflict.) Boys who continue to use physical aggression through their teenaged years are more likely than those who give up physical aggression to become involved in serious and violent offences as adults.

While incidents involving overt physical aggression usually decline during the teen years, acts of covert aggression—such as breaking rules, lying, skipping school or cheating—increase.

Young people who act aggressively—even within bounds that are considered normal and common for their age group—need to be made aware that their behaviours are not socially acceptable. *(In the next section, you will find a number of general strategies for preventing, reducing and managing normal aggression— strategies that have worked in treatment settings for children and youth.)*

How to manage "normal" aggression

An Ontario high-school art teacher was in the midst of giving a drawing lesson. Suddenly, she heard voices rising at the back of the class. Two boys began shouting swear words at each other. One of them pushed the other, tipping over a number of easels.

If you work or volunteer with young people, you have undoubtedly seen a number of incidents involving aggressive behaviour. Sometimes you may have known exactly what to do. At other times, you may have felt unsure about the best way to respond. The following strategies are intended to:
• help you prevent aggression among the young people you work with
• manage situations that involve aggressive behaviours
• discuss any incidents of aggression that do occur with the young people involved, in order to discourage similar incidents in the future.

Most of the approaches presented in this chapter are suitable for both children and adolescents, although you may have to adapt a few when working with the latter group. Most adolescents, for example, value privacy, so you will have to make sure you respect their privacy if you wish to gain their trust. Adolescents also need to feel that they are in control; they often tune out adults who give them direct orders. Therefore, make strong suggestions rather than giving orders. For example, rather than saying "Call your friend up right now and apologize," you could say, "You might want to call your friend and apologize for what happened. You might find that, if you call her, you two can work things out in a way that will suit you both."

Preventing aggression

The best way to reduce incidents of aggression among young people is to prevent them from occurring in the first place.

Preventing aggression takes some thought and care. You first need to become aware of what situations are likely to trigger aggressive behaviours, and then keep those situations from arising by using age-appropriate strategies. Successfully discouraging aggressive behaviour in young people also involves building solid and appropriate relationships with them, and creating a structured and secure environment. Here are a number of tips for doing that:

Set out clear expectations

At the start of a new relationship with young people, set out clear ground rules for their behaviour. These might include such simple regulations as "no swearing," "keep your hands and feet to yourselves" and "follow directions." You should also make it clear that those young people who do not follow your ground rules will face consequences; then make sure you follow through when the occasion arises.

Build rapport and be understanding

Working well with young people demands more than just maintaining order and discipline. It's also important to establish a bond with them based on trust and mutual respect. To do this, you will need to talk to them to get a sense of their thoughts, feelings and life experiences. You should also show concern and be ready to listen if they bring their own issues or problems to you. Consider finding out if there is an adult they respect and like, and why, and try to model some of those positive traits. Be aware of differences between the way you view the world and the way young people might view it, especially if they come from a background that is different from yours. In these ways, you might discover something about the risk and protective factors for aggression in the lives of the young people you are connected with, and come up with workable strategies for decreasing the risk factors and boosting the protective factors.

Also, be aware that family and environmental factors can play a role in how young people behave on a daily basis. For example, a child might arrive at school right after a family argument, or without a good night's sleep or a healthy breakfast.

Show cultural sensitivity

If you work in a setting in which young people come from different social, cultural and religious backgrounds, be sensitive to that fact. Keep in mind that some behaviours considered unusual or a cause for concern in one culture may be considered normal and acceptable in another. Avoid labelling and stereotyping.

Avoid negative talk

Adults often talk to each other about the children or youth with whom they work or volunteer, and unfortunately, the talk is sometimes negative. For example, a frustrated Grade 3 teacher may warn her school's Grade 4 teacher about an "impossible" child who'll be entering her class next year. Or a group home worker might tell a new staff member about the "hopeless" 13-year-old in the group.

Negative talk about young people can prejudice the views of adults, which can, in turn, prevent those young people from improving their behaviours. Having heard a discouraging report about a particular child, the Grade 4 teacher mentioned above might treat her differently from others in her class. She might, for example, be slower to praise the child—even though the Grade 3 teacher may not have given her accurate information, and the child's behaviour may have changed. In any case, children with behavioural concerns often need praise to encourage positive behaviours.

Avoid using negative words, facial expressions and tone of voice when talking directly to young people. Also, take care not to overreact emotionally to young people who present challenging behaviours. A high school teacher might be tempted to greet a student who's returning to school after being suspended with a comment such as, "So, what can we expect from you now?" But sarcastic comments will not encourage a young person to behave in socially acceptable ways.

Don't allow others to talk negatively about the children or youth you work with, either. Curb negative talk in a non-aggressive way by saying, for example, "It's not respectful to speak about young people in that way."

Don't assume or make judgments

Don't make any assumptions about young people based on what you may have heard from others. Your assumptions could spoil new relationships before they begin. Similarly, be ready to revise earlier judgments you yourself may have made. If you act on assumptions, you may discourage more positive behaviours, or not even notice when a young person's behaviour has begun to change for the better.

Be encouraging

Be positive. Offer praise and thanks for positive behaviours, rather than taking them for granted. For example, compliment young people when they do their schoolwork quietly or get along with peers. They may make light of your compliments, but don't let up. You can also offer encouragement in other ways, such as the following:

- Offer age-appropriate rewards for positive behaviours, such as healthy treats, stickers, free time, or praising notes to parents.
- Ask young people to do simple tasks (for example, "Can you please shut the door?"). Then thank and praise them when the tasks are done (for example, "Thanks, it was very helpful of you to do that."). This strategy encourages young people to develop respect for and comply with your requests.
- Talk positively about the specific behaviour of young people to their parents or other adults, while the young people are present. For example, say, "He concentrated very well in art class and produced a great painting," or "She was listening well during story time."
- Never make fun of the children or youth you encounter. Accept all their ideas and thoughts. If you ridicule them, especially in front of their peers, you can cause long-lasting emotional harm.
- Be flexible in your demands. If a young person is struggling in one area, reduce expectations around other schoolwork, chores or activities. Praise any accomplishment he or she does achieve and then gradually increase your expectations.

Avoid power struggles

All young people can be oppositional (verbally contrary or defiant) from time to time. They may argue, talk back and refuse to do what they are told. Children or youth who have been diagnosed with oppositional defiant disorder show these behaviours more often than the average.

Whenever possible, avoid getting into direct power struggles with young people—struggles in which you, for example, command them to do what they're told with the reason "because I said so." Direct power struggles are likely to provoke rather than discourage incidents of aggression. In such situations, both you and any young people involved are likely to lose your tempers. And the young people will not learn why you wished them to behave in a given way, nor will they be motivated to repeat the positive behaviour in the future. Rather, they will learn ways to aggravate you or "push your buttons."

Manage problems

Manage problems as they arise. If small problems are not tackled, they may build into bigger ones. If you need to tell a young person that he or she has done something wrong, do so quickly and quietly. Address problems in a firm, fair and consistent manner, and use mild consequences, such as time outs or loss of privileges, to discourage negative behaviours. Remember especially to watch your tone of voice when discussing negative behaviours and consequences. Do not raise your voice in anger, even if the young person becomes angry with you. Stay calm.

Offer options, but have a bottom line. For example, if a child refuses to do schoolwork, you could ask if he or she would like some help from a classmate, or suggest putting the problematic task aside for a while to work on other exercises. Make it clear, however, that the work needs to be done by a certain time.

Become aware of triggers

Become aware of the situations or stresses that trigger a young person to act up and behave aggressively. Some of these triggers might be revealed during initial conversations; others might only surface after you've known the child or youth for a while. Here are some common situations that may trigger aggressive behaviours in young people:
• a conflict with a peer
• a change in routine
• facing a task or expectation that is too challenging
• a bad mood, possibly caused by tiredness or hunger
• too many distractions in the environment
• being approached by an adult or authority figure in an unfavourable way, such as being shamed, ridiculed, embarrassed or put down.

Reduce the effect of, or eliminate, trigger situations

Once you identify the situations or stresses that trigger a young person to behave aggressively, try to minimize their impact. For example, you can reduce expectations when necessary, and then gradually increase them again over time; or if the trigger is a conflict between peers, try to find out what is causing the problem and help the young people to resolve it. Remember to use a non-confrontational tone of voice when making requests.

In classroom settings, there are certain well-identified times when young people are most likely to behave aggressively: during seatwork periods (quiet times when students work on their own) and during transitions between activities. Ways to reduce the likelihood of aggressive behaviour during seatwork periods include:
• interacting often with students
• using rewards to promote good behaviour
• cutting back on the time allotted if problems begin to arise.

To prevent problems during transitions, try:
• warning students in advance about any change in routine
• communicating clear procedures for student behaviour during transitions, and remind students of these just before transitions are about to occur
• monitoring students closely during transitions.

Get young people involved

Help the young people you are involved with to play an active role in preventing incidents of aggression. For example, ask them questions such as:
- "How can I help you behave in positive ways?"
- "What doesn't help you behave in positive ways? What don't you like?"
- "When you aren't having a great day, how can I help you make it better?"
- "It's okay to feel angry or frustrated—but how do you usually deal with these feelings?"
- "What do you think are some helpful ways to deal with anger or frustration? How can we avoid unhelpful reactions?"

Develop strategies to help young people manage their emotions

Work with young people to help them develop the skills necessary to manage emotions that can lead to aggressive outbursts. *(See Chapter 7 for practical advice on how to incorporate anger management training, problem-solving skills training and social skills training into your work with young people.)*

Use positive reinforcement

Whenever possible, praise and reward positive social behaviours. Praising positive behaviour when it occurs is one of the best ways to encourage children and youth to behave positively in the future.

Be prepared to manage incidents involving aggression

The next section provides advice on how to do this.

Managing aggression

Even if you work hard to prevent it, if you work with young people you will likely face aggressive behaviour at some point. The strategies described below have worked to lessen the intensity of aggressive behaviours among children and youth in treatment settings. These strategies are designed to help you diffuse a situation or calm a young person; find out what caused the outburst and address the cause; and build better relationships with young people to find out if they need special help.

Control your body language and tone of voice

Through our gestures, postures and facial expressions we express physical, mental or emotional states and communicate them non-verbally to others. Our body language and tone of voice can emphasize the message of our spoken words—or it can contradict that message.

If you're confronted with a young person who is behaving aggressively or making threats, be sure to control your own body language and tone of voice. Certain types of body language and tones of voice can disturb some young people and cause their aggression levels to rise.

Do:
• keep your voice calm and even
• keep your facial expression as neutral as possible to avoid showing emotion
• maintain eye contact to show you are giving attention, but don't insist that the young person maintain eye contact with you
• make sure the person has enough physical space
• if you need to, take a few seconds to calm yourself down before interacting.

Don't:
• shake or wave your fingers in the young person's face
• put your hands on your hips
• glare, sneer, scowl or frown
• get too close
• yell or sigh in exasperation
• slam doors, books or other objects.

Stay calm

When you are confronted with a child or youth who is behaving aggressively, you may find yourself becoming angry or frustrated. These feelings are natural, but if you express them you may further disturb the young person. Approach calmly, and try to get the young person to focus on his or her own feelings. Use simple statements, such as "It looks like you're having a hard time. It doesn't need to be like that." Remember that when you approach young people who are behaving aggressively, they will often become verbally aggressive toward you. They may yell or swear; ignore it. Don't take the negative statements made to you at such a time personally. Also, don't try to solve the problem or conflict that led to the aggressive behaviour while a young person is acting aggressively toward you. Focus first on letting the person know that you care about him or her, are concerned about what is happening and are there to help.

Offer a way out

Offer a young person a way out of the situation. Give clear choices, with safe limitations. In this way, you allow the young person to retain a feeling of control. You can give the person an opportunity to retain his or her self-esteem. For example, you might ask, "Would you like to sit over there for a while to gather your thoughts?"

Discourage bystanders

When a young person is acting up, ask peers who may be watching to leave the setting and continue with their activities. For example, if a conflict between students erupts in a school hallway, direct students who are not involved politely but firmly to their next class—or draw the students who are arguing away from the crowd into an empty classroom. The reaction of a crowd can encourage some young people to increase the aggressiveness of their behaviour.

Don't make threats

Don't give warnings about consequences that you are not prepared to follow through on. Young people will not respond well to warnings if they have learned through past experience that they will not necessarily have to face them. When a young person is showing very aggressive behaviour, resist the temptation to threaten him or her with a consequence that you know you cannot deliver or that is unreasonably severe.

Don't make predictions

Saying, "You always do this when..." reinforces negative behaviours.

Wait for the right moment

Wait to talk to a young person about inappropriate behaviours until after an incident involving aggression is over, when everyone has calmed down.

Maintain safety

Make sure that the young people and staff members who are present during an incident involving aggression are safe at all times. If you can't control the situation, be prepared to call for help from another staff member, an administrator or the police, depending on what is happening.

Deal appropriately with threats

In most cases, children or youth who make threats don't carry them out. You can therefore use many of the tips listed elsewhere in this section to deal with threats. Your main goal will be to get a young person making threats to focus on the way he or she is feeling, and away from any target of aggression. You can do this by making comments such as, "You must be feeling really bad to say something like that. What's going on?"

It is not always easy to predict whether or not a young person will carry out a threat, even if you have successfully managed the crisis during which the threat was uttered. To determine if the threat is likely to be carried out, think about the past behaviour of the person who made it. Young people who have behaved aggressively, damaged property, set fires, harmed animals or shown other conduct problems in the past are more likely than average to carry out a threat *(see the chart in Chapter 5 showing behaviours that are cause for concern)*. In such cases, you may need to contact a mental health service provider or the police, depending on the situation.

Always take matters seriously if a young person threatens:
• to hurt or kill someone
• to hurt or kill himself or herself
• to damage or destroy property.

After an incident is over

Once an incident involving aggression is over—and everyone has calmed down— it is time to talk things over with the young people who were involved. You can then help them gain an understanding of what caused the incident and come up with ways to prevent future problems. Here are some tips for working with young people after an incident:
• Talk to each of the young people in private. Be respectful. Ask them what they thought happened and how the incident may have affected others. Listen to all sides of the story.
• Ask the young people if they would be willing to hear about what you saw during the incident. Then give them each the chance to comment on whether they think your impressions are correct or not.
• Talk about your concerns regarding the aggressive behaviour.
• Follow through with consequences that have been previously discussed, such as a loss of privileges.
• Explore problem-solving strategies together. Help the young people see what they could have done differently. Point out approaches you may have already talked about. Talk about how they might use those approaches in the future.
• If young people ask you to act as a mediator in a conflict with a peer, be available and neutral.

WENDEL'S STORY
Normal aggression

Wendel was an easygoing 15-year-old who enjoyed going to an after-school community drop-in program. One day, he and his friends were playing a game at the drop-in centre, and he lost. The drop-in leader asked him to sit out, as was expected, and wait for the next round of play. Wendel refused. Then he became angry. He picked up a chair and smashed it to the floor.

The drop-in leader easily managed to diffuse the situation, calm Wendel down and talk to him. In the course of their conversation, Wendel admitted he had had a bad day. He had had a fight with his parents that morning, and at school he had found out he'd failed a test.

The drop-in leader had known Wendel for several months and recognized that it was unusual for Wendel to behave aggressively. He and Wendel were able to talk about socially acceptable ways to cope with having a bad day. The leader didn't think Wendel's behaviour reflected a more serious problem for several reasons. First, Wendel had never acted that way before. Second, he had calmed down easily and could talk about the event soon afterward. Third, Wendel usually got along well with his friends, teachers and other adults, and showed no conduct problems or other behaviours to be concerned about. *(For examples of behaviours to be concerned about, see Chapter 5.)*

Chapter 5

When is aggression a concern?

Overview of aggression by age group

If you work or volunteer with young people, you will probably witness, and have to manage, situations involving aggressive behaviour—some minor, some more serious. At times you may wonder whether a particular child or youth has a problem with aggression that needs specialized intervention.

The information provided in the chart that follows will help you decide. The left column of the chart summarizes the information discussed in Chapter 4: it presents an overview of aggressive behaviours that experts consider normal for specific phases of young people's development. The right column presents aggressive behaviours that experts think are of more concern: these behaviours can indicate that a child or youth has a problem with aggression that should be identified and treated by a health care provider with special training.

Infants' and toddlers' behaviours (ages 0–2)

Normal behaviours	Behaviours to be concerned about
• Often display physical aggression, such as biting, hitting or pushing • Have temper tantrums, starting around age 18–24 months, three to six times a week	• Are very fussy and irritable • Have irregular sleeping or eating patterns • Demand a lot of attention • Don't seek comfort from parents

Preschoolers' behaviours (ages 3–5)

Normal behaviours	Behaviours to be concerned about
• Show some aggressive behaviours, such as grabbing toys, pushing and kicking • Begin some verbal aggression or name calling • Show more aggression toward siblings than peers • Generally respond to reprimands	• Are overactive and impulsive, and appear fearless • Have many lengthy temper tantrums in a day, or can't be easily calmed • Have aggressive outbursts for no apparent reason • Get frustrated easily • Don't seem attached to parents • Often refuse to comply with teachers' or parents' requests • Often fight with peers • Try to harm teachers or other adults

Girls

• Start to show social aggression

School-aged children's behaviours (ages 6–11)

Normal behaviours	Behaviours to be concerned about
• Refuse to follow instructions or rules at times, with minimal consequences (for example, nobody is hurt, routines are not seriously affected and the behaviour can be managed)	• Have temper tantrums
	• Have problems paying attention or concentrating
• Show more verbal aggression	• Often get into fights or use physical force to get things
• Have more frequent conflicts with siblings	• Are often disruptive in class
	• Lose their temper easily
• Have minor conflicts with other children	• Are preoccupied with violent games or TV shows
	• Damage or destroy property
	• Use alcohol or other drugs
	• Set fires
	• Harm animals
	• Seek out aggressive children and are rejected by other peers
	• Constantly disobey or argue with adults

Boys

• Engage in rough-and-tumble play— lots of pretend fighting	• Engage in extreme forms of aggression, as described above
• Show more risk-taking behaviour than girls	• Display frequent aggression toward girls

Girls

• Use social aggression more, particularly on entering early adolescence	• Frequently engage in physical aggression
• Use physical aggression less than boys	• Are often aggressive toward boys

Adolescents' behaviours (age 12 and older)

Normal behaviours

- During early adolescence, may have angry outbursts or temper tantrums (such as swearing, cursing or slamming doors)

- Have fewer outbursts by later adolescence

- Use covert aggression (such as lying) more

Behaviours to be concerned about

- Don't respect others' rights or feelings

- Use aggression to solve problems

- Resist authority

- Skip school or drop out

- Do poorly in school

- Have substance use problems

- Destroy property

- Run away from home

- Have friends who are aggressive

- Join a gang and take part in illegal activities

Boys

- Engage in less physical aggression than during elementary-school years

- Use aggression directly, through confrontation

- Are frequently aggressive toward girls

Girls

- Continue to use verbal or social aggression rather than physical aggression

- May resort to physical aggression if attacked

- Display frequent physical aggression

- Are frequently aggressive toward boys

Determining if there is a serious problem

If you are trying to determine whether or not a young person has a serious problem with aggression, ask yourself the following series of key questions. You may need to speak to the young person's parents (or other adults who have worked with the person) to get some of the answers.

What type of behaviour is the young person displaying?

- Does the young person show any behaviours of concern for his or her age group *(see the chart on the previous pages)*?
- If so, how many? (The more such behaviours displayed, the greater the likelihood that the young person needs special help.)

- Are you concerned about the young person's behaviour for any other reasons besides aggression?

How severe is the behaviour?

- Is it difficult to calm the young person down after an outburst?

- Does the behaviour persist despite your best efforts to talk to the child or youth, to set fair and consistent discipline measures, or to use any other strategies to intervene?

- Does the behaviour appear to be getting worse?

How often does the behaviour occur?

- Does it occur every day, every week or every month?

What triggers the behaviour?

- Does the young person explode at situations that don't bother other young people?

- Does he or she explode for no obvious reason?

How long has the behaviour been occurring?

- Has the young person been behaving aggressively for a long time?

- Did he or she display any behaviours of concern *(listed in the chart on the previous pages)* at an earlier age?

Has the young person's behaviour had any serious consequences?

• Has he or she injured himself or anyone else?

Has the behaviour affected the young person's daily life, relationships or school performance?

• Does he or she take part in everyday household activities?

• Does the young person's behaviour lead to conflicts with parents or siblings?

• Does the behaviour lead to conflicts with peers?

• Does the young person have problems making friends?

• Do all the young person's friends behave aggressively or anti-socially?

• Does he or she have any learning problems, either long-standing or new?

• Have his or her school grades fallen?

• Does the young person's behaviour lead to conflicts with teachers?
  Does it disturb other students?

Think about each answer carefully, and take into account the portrait created when you consider all the answers together. Depending on the situation, you may find it more or less difficult to decide whether a particular young person needs help.

As you consider your decision, remember that, as noted at the end of Chapter 1, most of us react to situations from the perspective of our own culture and background. How you analyze the answers to the above questions will therefore be influenced by your cultural and social background, as well as by your life experiences. If you take some time to reflect upon your own background and how it might influence your perspective, you may be less likely to jump to inappropriate conclusions.

Taking the time to identify young people who are having problems with aggressive behaviour is worthwhile. You may then have the chance to guide their parents to find the right kind of treatment. The earlier a young person with an aggression problem is identified and receives help, the greater the chance that the chosen treatment will have lasting benefits.

JOHN'S STORY
When a young person needs help

John, aged 14, was a shy, straight-A student who had a few close friends. He was raised in a close-knit Chinese family. John's parents were both successful professionals. They told him they expected him to become a doctor and encouraged him to study hard at school. While John did do well academically, he also had a passion for sports and music. When he tried to tell his parents about these interests, they did not support him. Instead, they criticized and discouraged him. They harshly criticized him when he developed an interest in rap music.

John became frustrated with his parents. He began to hit them. Over the course of several months, he hit them both a number of times. John's parents were very upset by his behaviour and contacted his school guidance counsellor for help.

For several reasons, the guidance counsellor thought that John and his family would benefit from family therapy. John's aggressive reaction to his parents' disapproval was extreme and unusual for a person of his age. His behaviour also had a strong negative impact on his family's life, upsetting his younger siblings, damaging his relationship with his parents, and causing his parents severe stress. On the other hand, John's parents were harshly critical of his interests. John's parents agreed with the guidance counsellor's informal assessment and made an appointment to go with John to speak with a psychologist.

(For a discussion of how John's aggression problems were treated, see Chapter 7.)

Chapter 6

Assessment

Perhaps you have decided that a young person with whom you work or volunteer has a problem with aggression and needs help. To reach that conclusion, you probably spent some time considering the person's behaviour. You might have consulted the chart in Chapter 5 and thought about answers to the questions listed there. You probably weighed the young person's risk factors against the protective factors *(outlined in Chapter 3)* and spoke to the person's parents and teachers. By using these or other tools to consider whether the person has a problem with aggression, you have conducted a kind of evaluation, one that some experts call an *informal assessment*.

Formal *clinical assessments* are also evaluations. They can be conducted by a number of different kinds of health care providers, such as psychiatrists, family doctors, nurses, psychologists or social workers. Assessments involve the use of tested methods to understand young people's behaviour with respect to their families, school environments and peer relationships.

A health care provider making a clinical assessment may also make a *diagnosis*. In this case, the person making the assessment considers the young person's behaviour to determine whether he or she has a mental health disorder that has been classified in the American Psychiatric Association's *Diagnostic and Statistical Manual of Mental Disorders* (DSM). *(For a fuller discussion of mental health disorders and their relationship to aggression, see Chapter 8.)*

The goal of an assessment is to develop a plan of action to reduce or eliminate the problems with aggression being faced by the young person and his or her family, and to promote and strengthen their well-being.

Navigating the system

If you think a young person has an aggression problem requiring special help, your first step is to speak to his or her parents. During this conversation, you can let the parents know that you think it would be helpful for their child to have an assessment. If the parents are willing, they can begin the process of getting help for their child by making an appointment to see their family doctor. If the family doesn't have a regular doctor, they can make an appointment to see a doctor at a clinic.

Family doctors are often the first health care providers that families turn to when they are coping with a mental health or behavioural problem. The family doctor might make an assessment, or might refer the family to a psychiatrist, psychologist or social worker who has a good clinical understanding of young people and aggression, and up-to-date knowledge of the best practices in this area.

Once you have spoken with a young person's parents, your role may end. The parents may, however, ask you to stay involved as an advocate or a case manager. An *advocate* is someone who speaks out on behalf of a young person, finds appropriate services and looks for alternatives if one plan doesn't work out. A *case manager* knows the young person and is aware of all the services he or she is using, and can act as a liaison among different health care providers, if needed. The same person—a parent, the family doctor or you—could fill both of these roles.

During your conversations with a young person's family, remember to show sensitivity and to recognize that some families may prefer to look for help within their own cultural or religious communities. Also, be aware that some parents may not be open to the idea of an assessment.

What an assessment involves

Conducting an assessment takes time. It involves careful consideration of many interrelated aspects of the young person's life and past and present behaviour.

During the early stages, the person conducting the assessment will want to look at the educational, medical and legal records of the young person concerned. If learning problems are discovered or suspected, it may be recommended that the young person undergo intellectual or educational tests. These tests measure academic skills, age-appropriate grasp of concepts, and social skills. *(For a discussion of IQ and IQ tests, see Chapter 3.)*

Three major activities are involved in an assessment:
• conducting interviews
• using standardized checklists and rating scales
• directly observing how the young person behaves in a variety of settings.

Each of these activities is discussed in more detail below.

Conducting interviews

Interviews are generally conducted with the young person and with his or her parents, teachers and possibly other adults who know the person well, such as extended family members (for example, grandparents, aunts or uncles) and peers. Each interview delves as deeply as possible into the life and history of the young person being assessed, including:
• his or her birth and related events
• the ages at which key physical and emotional skills developed
• the ages, occupations, marital status and medical, educational and mental health histories of family members
• the personal and social skills of the young person.

In the case of adolescents, the interviews will include questions about the youth's substance use. The aim is to learn about all the risk and protective factors for aggression in the young person's life.

Through the interviews, the person conducting the assessment gains an understanding of the aggression problem and its triggers, forms of expression and consequences This allows the person to determine whether the aggression is normal or something to be concerned about, and to help decide what kind of treatment will most likely be helpful.

Checklists and rating scales

Common tools used during an assessment include problem-focused checklists and rating scales. These tools contain standardized lists of questions that can help determine whether a young person's behaviour is normal for his or her age and level of development or is something to be concerned about. The young person's parents and teachers (and sometimes the young person) are asked whether various behaviours are present or absent, and how frequent and intense these behaviours are.

One of the most commonly used checklists for assessing problems involving aggression, as well as other anti-social behaviours, is the Child Behaviour Checklist 4-18 (CBCL), a 118-item questionnaire. Another widely used tool is the Diagnostic Interview Schedule for Children Version IV (DISC-IV). A newer scale is the Carolina Child Checklist (CCC), which was developed specifically to measure the risk and protective factors related to aggressive behaviour in children aged six to 12.

Direct observation

During the assessment process, the behaviour of the young person is observed in a variety of settings, including at home, in school and at a clinic. The purpose of direct observation is to see first-hand how the young person interacts with family members, teachers and peers, and to assess the extent to which his or her behaviour matches that described in the interviews.

Direct observation has drawbacks, however. For one thing, young people may alter their day-to-day behaviour if they are aware they are being watched. For another, it may be impossible using this method to detect acts of covert aggression, such as lying, cheating, stealing and setting fires. Finally, a young person's behaviour may be difficult to understand, and the person conducting the assessment may need to see how it develops over time before reaching a conclusion.

Pros and cons of an assessment

An assessment can help dispel any misconceptions or assumptions that others have made about a young person. It can also help to get a referral for more specialized help if necessary. In some regions, an assessment is required in order to get funding for special services from a school board (for example, for a special education teacher to help out in the classroom).

However, assessments are imperfect and subjective. Different health care providers assessing the same young person can come to different conclusions. As a result, parents may want to have their child assessed by more than one person.

There are many reasons why the outcomes of assessments may vary. For example, the cultural beliefs of the person doing the assessment may influence the diagnosis—especially when the young person comes from a culture that is different from their own. To address this issue, some health care providers have begun to specialize in more culturally sensitive approaches to assessment. They try to better understand the behaviour of the young people being assessed within a larger context, by exploring their socio-cultural backgrounds. This knowledge can help people conducting assessments:

• interpret what they learn
• choose the right tools
• fully explain the results of an assessment to a family
• reassure parents and young people about why they are suggesting a particular approach
• recommend the most effective treatment.

At times it is possible for young people to be assessed by health care providers who share their socio-cultural background.

The health care provider strives to make as accurate an assessment as possible by talking to all the people who know a young person well, and by using questionnaires that have been shown to give meaningful answers about behaviour. After an assessment is complete, the next step is to develop a workable plan of action, designed to reduce the negative impact of risk factors and to strengthen the positive impact of protective factors related to aggression and other behaviours. *(In the following chapter, you can read about some of the most common treatments for aggression.)*

Chapter 7

Prevention and intervention

Identifying risk and protective factors not only helps us understand the factors leading to aggression among young people, but also offers a model for developing ways to help young people who behave aggressively. Researchers have developed some programs to reduce the negative impact of certain risk factors, and developed others to strengthen the positive effects of protective factors. Often, these two aims are combined.

In the next section you will find a discussion of some of the most effective treatments and interventions developed to prevent, reduce or eliminate aggression in young people. The interventions are presented in three main groups: those related to individual factors (such as temperament or social and personal skills), family factors (such as parental disciplinary methods) and environmental factors (such as bullying at school).

A variety of health care providers—including family doctors, nurses, pediatricians, psychiatrists, psychologists and social workers—can counsel young people and provide the treatments discussed below. Their respective services are offered in a wide variety of settings, including schools, youth clinics, mental health treatment centres (including psychiatric hospitals), substance use treatment centres (including residential and day-treatment centres), private practices and correctional institutions.

The cost of these services can vary. Some may be covered by provincial or employee insurance plans, or may be available on a sliding-scale basis. In other cases, clients are required to pay the full cost. Sometimes a young person may have to go on a waiting list to receive this kind of treatment from a health care provider, especially one whose treatment costs are totally covered by insurance plans.

Some of the following interventions, such as training in anger management or problem-solving skills, include methods for encouraging behavioural changes that can also be taught by other qualified people. Consider including some of these methods in your own work with young people.

Interventions that target individual risk and protective factors

Cognitive-behavioural therapy

Health care providers use the word *therapy* to describe a variety of treatments for both physical and mental health problems. Different therapists (including psychiatrists, psychologists and social workers) may offer different types of therapy, depending on their training and views. Some family doctors or general practitioners also offer therapy for mental health problems, but they may not have specialized training in this area.

Many health care providers consider cognitive-behavioural therapy (CBT) to be the best way to treat some of the most common mental health problems, including aggression. CBT focuses on helping people become aware of their automatic negative thoughts, attitudes, expectations and beliefs, and to understand how these negative thinking patterns contribute to unhealthy feelings and behaviours. Qualified therapists can help people change negative thinking patterns into positive ones, thus changing both the feelings and the behaviours. Through CBT, people learn to have more control over their moods and actions by having more control over their thoughts.

For example, CBT can help young people improve their self-esteem by turning negative thoughts about themselves into positive thoughts. (As noted in Chapter 3, high self-esteem is a protective factor that can help keep young people from developing aggressive behaviour.) CBT can also help young people who often feel angry to understand the sources of their anger, and can teach them to have a different perspective so that they don't feel as angry.

Social skills training

Social skills training teaches young people skills that enable them to have positive relations with peers and adults. Having good social skills involves knowing how to manage emotions and behaviours, communicating in socially acceptable ways and understanding the feelings of others. Social skills training for young people can include teaching them how to:
• greet others politely when they meet
• say "please" and "thank you"
• ask permission when they want something
• start conversations
• take turns
• listen during conversations
• apologize.

In addition, this type of training may teach young people to consider how others think and feel in social situations, and to correctly read social signals.

Health care providers or counsellors who offer social skills training programs use a variety of methods, such as role-playing, to teach the abilities listed above. For example, they might ask young people to pretend that they are meeting a new classmate for the first time, or that they would like to hand in an assignment late to their teacher. At the beginning of the role play, the counsellor might act out the young people's parts for them, showing them both appropriate and inappropriate social behaviours. The young people then act out the parts themselves. As they do so, the counsellor coaches them and gives them feedback, including encouragement and praise when they have played their parts in socially acceptable ways. One benefit of role-playing is that it can help people expand their awareness of how others might feel in different situations.

Counsellors may also give homework assignments in which the young people practise the skills they have learned. Some social skills programs involve providing the parents with instruction so that they too can successfully guide their children. Sometimes counsellors may, with the permission of both their young clients and the parents, tell teachers when they are working with students in their class. This allows the teachers to reinforce the social skills lessons at school, by encouraging and praising appropriate social behaviours.

If you are working with young people to teach them good social skills, you must be patient and supportive. Changing old habits is never an easy task for anyone, at any age. The struggle, however, is well worth it. Building good social skills helps young people improve their relationships with parents, teachers, other adults and peers. Having positive relationships is a protective factor for aggression.

Problem-solving skills training

As its name suggests, problem-solving skills training was designed by psychologists to teach people a series of clearly defined steps that they can use to solve problems, including those that arise in school, work, social or family situations. Counsellors use this type of training to help young people who behave aggressively to learn to think aloud about the problems they may be having with others, and then to follow certain steps to successfully manage the problems.

According to psychologists, these are the main steps to take to solve any problem:
• Define the problem.
• Think up alternative solutions and consider the pros and cons of each.
• Choose the best solution.
• Make a plan.
• Carry out the plan.
• Evaluate the outcome.

During a problem-solving skills training program, a counsellor might first model this way of thinking about problems for a client, perhaps using an example from personal experience. For instance:

> I was really angry at my friend the other day, because he hung up the phone on me so quickly. I thought of calling him back right away and yelling at him. Instead, I decided to wait and cool off a little while. I'm glad I did, because my friend called me the next day to say that he didn't feel well, and that's why he had hung up so fast.

This kind of modelling can help young people learn good problem-solving strategies. They can also practise these strategies in role-playing games that imitate real-life situations.

Some counsellors also use role-playing to help young people recognize the ways—both positive and negative—in which they usually behave when confronting a problem. Clients are encouraged to consider their use of eye contact, loudness and tone of voice, and gestures—and then decide whether each behaviour helps solve their problems or makes them worse.

Problem-solving skills training can help young people to recognize what situations usually trigger their aggressive behaviours, and then to develop a plan to respond to those situations in more socially acceptable ways. Having good problem-solving skills is a protective factor for aggression.

If you work or volunteer with young people, you may wish to incorporate some elements of problem-solving skills training into your curriculum or program.

Anger management training

Anger is a normal human emotion. It can range in intensity from feelings of mild irritation to full-blown rage. Counsellors who offer anger management training teach people first how to recognize their feelings of anger, and the contexts in which those feelings tend to occur. They encourage clients to discuss the situations that trigger their anger, and teach them to understand how their bodies react physically. Feelings of anger, like feelings of danger, trigger the human body to prepare to fight or take flight. Heart rate and blood pressure rise, as do levels of certain hormones, such as adrenaline.

Anger management training can help young people and their families learn ways to reduce their feelings of anger and the physical reactions that these emotions can generate. The training is based on the idea that while people can't always eliminate or avoid the situations that make them angry, they can learn to control their reactions. By learning how to control themselves through this kind of training, young people may be able to prevent incidents involving reactive aggression.

Counsellors offering this training encourage clients to talk about the thoughts they usually have when they are angry and the actions that they take as a result. They then teach methods that people can use to control feelings of anger—before their emotions take control of them. Some of these methods involve relaxation techniques, such as counting to 10, taking deep breaths, repeating words like "calm down" or "take it easy," imagining a relaxing situation or doing slow stretching. Counsellors ask clients to practise these relaxation techniques so they can draw upon them easily when they are in a tense situation and are beginning to have feelings of anger.

Another aspect of anger management training is teaching people to change their usual thinking patterns. Young people who are feeling angry might curse. They might say things to themselves or others, such as, "I hate my friend. I'm never going to talk to her again. I'm going to get back at her." Anger management counsellors use modelling and role-playing to teach young people to replace thoughts such as these with calmer and more rational ones, such as "I'm frustrated with my friend right now. It's understandable that I'm upset with her. But it's not the end of the world and getting angry is not going to help."

The final steps of anger management training can involve teaching clients problem-solving skills *(discussed in the previous section),* so they can learn how to more calmly identify a problem that is making them angry, and resolve it to the best of their ability. Young people taking this training need to learn to accept that although not all problems have simple solutions, problems can be managed in socially appropriate ways that do not involve aggression.

Anger management training can be incorporated into youth programs or school curricula. Bookstores and libraries carry books on the subject from which you can get specific ideas for teaching the above techniques.

Attributional retraining

Some young people are quick to assume that others have hostile intentions toward them, even when there is no real evidence of hostility *(see the discussion of social signals in Chapter 3).* Youth in this situation can benefit from a specific type of therapy called *attributional retraining.* This approach teaches people how to correctly interpret others' intentions—for example, by showing them how to read others' facial expressions and gestures.

Counsellors can also encourage young people to talk about the thoughts and feelings they usually have when they are in contact with others, to recognize when they are making wrong assumptions and to consider the kinds of actions that they usually take as a result. The idea underlying attributional retraining is that if people do not automatically believe that others are "out to get them," they will be less likely to act aggressively. Attributional retraining programs are most successful with those over the age of 10.

Interventions that target family risk and protective factors

Parent management skills training

Parenting is perhaps the most difficult of all jobs: it comes with no pay and tremendous responsibility, and most adults receive little or no formal training for it. No one usually teaches parents how to nurture, support, guide and educate a child to become a capable adult. Most of us muddle along, generally tending to treat our children the way our parents treated us.

Psychologists have researched different parenting styles. Their studies show that the ways in which parents treat their children can either increase or decrease the likelihood that young people will show problem behaviours, including aggression. For example, parents may not realize that the use of too harsh, too lax, or inconsistent discipline can increase the probability that their children will behave aggressively. So can a lack of proper supervision *(see the discussion in Chapter 3 of level of supervision as a risk factor for aggression).*

Research has also provided psychologists with the foundation for developing parent management skills training (PMST) programs. PMST programs are designed to help parents and others develop the skills to manage children's behaviour effectively, and to cope with specific problems and disorders in children and adolescents. These programs can inform parents about strategies that have been proven to encourage young people's emotional and intellectual development. They can also assist parents in helping children cope with a divorce or other family crisis. PMST programs are designed to enable parents to change the ways in which they interact with their children, based on the understanding that the children's behaviour will improve as a result. PMST programs are most effective for parents who have children under the age of 12.

PMST programs can teach parents how to:
• observe, identify and manage children's problem behaviours
• set clear and consistent rules
• give instructions appropriately
• encourage appropriate behaviours by giving young people
  positive attention and reinforcement
• not give harsh punishments (such as spanking or belting)
  for negative behaviours
• discourage negative behaviours with mild consequences,
  such as time outs or the loss of privileges
• ignore less serious behaviours
• supervise children appropriately.

Counsellors use a variety of techniques when teaching these skills, including role-playing and exercises (some of which the parents might be asked to practise on their own, outside of the training sessions). Some counsellors offer PMST on its own, while others give it in combination with another form of therapy. It may be offered in private homes or in clinics, to individuals, couples or groups.

Studies have shown that PMST leads to improved behaviour among the children of parents who have received it. The training also reduces stress and depression in parents and increases their sense of effectiveness and confidence. PMST programs have the greatest chance of success if other problems that exist for the parents are addressed at the same time. Also, for the programs to be effective, parents must also be willing to make a long-term commitment of their time and energy, even though they may sometimes find this difficult because of other stresses.

You may know people who might benefit from taking a PMST program. If so, you can assure them that the program is not for "bad parents," nor is it specifically for the parents of children with serious psychological or behavioural problems. PMST can be worthwhile for any parents, as it can help them to do the best job possible.

Family therapy

Family therapy is a broad term that can incorporate CBT, solution-focused therapy, PMST, anger management training, problem-solving skills training, conflict management techniques or any other approaches that a therapist thinks will help families to make changes for the better. Family therapists consider each family's culture and values to ensure that what they do together is relevant and meaningful.

Family therapy focuses on helping families change their patterns of interaction to improve overall family cohesion, harmony and satisfaction. It aims to develop mutual understanding and improve communication among family members, without placing the blame for problems on any one person. Family therapy can help family members understand the ways in which a problem, such as aggression, can both affect and be affected by the family system. Some parents, for example, might turn to aggression to solve their own problems; their children will thus be more prone to behave aggressively than those raised by parents who solve their conflicts by other means.

Family therapy can help guide all family members to find fair, practical and non-violent solutions to conflicts and problems. It has been clinically shown that involving the whole family improves outcomes and increases the likelihood that young people will remain in treatment. It has also been shown that addressing the family system is integral to bringing about significant change in young people—perhaps because, of all the social systems that young people play a role in, the family system has the most impact on them.

During family therapy sessions, therapists encourage family members to speak about issues that may be troubling them. They make sure all family members get their say, while helping them sort through comments, issues and feelings. Different family therapists employ different methods, approaches and styles. Some choose to play a neutral role, while others intervene more. Therapists often focus on helping family members to develop more effective ways to get their points across and to understand the needs and feelings of other members. Through advice and modelling, they encourage everyone in the family to listen to one another and to express their feelings openly and honestly—though in ways that will not provoke feelings of anger in their listeners. When working with a family in which a young person is behaving aggressively, a therapist will try to help family members understand and cope, and act in a manner that will encourage the person to reduce the aggressive behaviour.

When working with families in which children show seriously delinquent behaviours, family therapists sometimes prefer a shorter-term, solution-focused approach. This approach is based upon the idea that to reduce severe aggression among young people you must first motivate them, and their families, to want to change.

During sessions, therapists motivate families by first uncovering each member's unique positive strengths (protective factors). They then help everyone in the family build on these strengths to enhance self-esteem. They encourage families to have hope for the future and to believe that they can improve their situation—even if the improvements come in small steps.

The next step is usually to help the family develop and launch a long-term behaviour change plan. The change plan is specific, culturally appropriate and tailored to match the unique characteristics of each family member.

In the final stages of many types of family therapy, therapists work with families to maintain change and prevent relapses. To do this, they may link families with community resources, and may help them deal with schools, the mental health system and, if necessary, the juvenile justice system.

Family therapy is offered in a variety of settings, including schools, homes, clinics, health and mental health institutions and private offices. Therapsits may work with families on a short- or long-term basis. They sometimes see whole families together; at other times they might work with members individually or in subgroups.

In certain cases, however, a therapist may decide that family therapy would not be helpful, and that it would be best to treat a young person alone. For example, if a young person has been physically, sexually and/or emotionally abused, the therapist may feel that having family members present in counselling sessions could hurt, rather than help, the young person.

JOHN'S STORY
How John was helped

In Chapter 5, we met 14-year-old John. Upset by his parents' disapproval of his interest in music and sports, John had hit them several times. On the advice of a school guidance counsellor, John's parents made an appointment for him to speak with a psychologist and have an assessment.

During the assessment, the psychologist used all the methods discussed in Chapter 6 to get to know and understand John. He also considered his risk and protective factors with respect to aggression: John had a high IQ, did well at school, had good relationships with his teachers and peers, and had hobbies that gave him enjoyment—all of which are protective factors. However, he and his parents did not communicate well—a risk factor for aggression, especially during a young person's teen years. John also had a low tolerance for frustration, another risk factor for aggression.

The psychologist recommended that John undergo anger management training (*discussed earlier in this chapter*) to help him understand the source of his frustration and anger and to communicate his feelings in more socially acceptable ways. The psychologist also engaged John's entire family in family therapy (*see the previous section in this chapter*) to help them learn better ways of expressing their views to each other. He helped John's parents set clear and realistic limits and expectations for John considering his age, stage of development and personal wishes. With the psychologist's help, they were able to convey these to John, allowing for discussion and negotiation so that he would be able to feel some control over his situation while recognizing his parents' authority. Gradually, John's aggressive behaviour toward his parents stopped, and the family learned how to recognize and accept each other's choices and values.

The Arson Prevention Program for Children

The Arson Prevention Program for Children (TAPP-C) was developed in the early 1990s by the Centre for Addiction and Mental Health, the Office of the Fire Marshal of Ontario and Toronto Fire Services, to help children and youth who inappropriately light, plan or threaten to light any kind of fire. Most young people begin inappropriate involvement with fire in their homes. TAPP-C therefore works with both young people and their families to come up with solutions to prevent inappropriate and potentially dangerous fire involvement. As one part of TAPP-C, a PMST program with trained mental health counsellors helps parents devise, and stick to, fire safety rules for the family. Counsellors also help the young people come up with their own ways of controlling fire-related impulses and behaviours. Another component of the program involves collaboration with fire service educators, who provide home safety checks and fire safety education.

Many young people who set fires have other behavioural problems, so TAPP-C also connects such young people with counsellors for additional treatment and support.

EVAN'S STORY
Helping a boy who plays with fire

Evan was a 15-year-old boy who lived at home with his mother and older brother and sister. Everyone in the family, including Evan, smoked cigarettes and carried matches and lighters. Evan's older brother enjoyed playing with fire and taught Evan how to do several tricks with his cigarette lighter. At school, Evan attracted the attention of his friends by doing these and other risk-taking tricks.

One day another boy made some rude comments about Evan's girlfriend, and Evan lit the boy's gym bag on fire in retaliation. By the time the fire department arrived, thousands of dollars of damage to the school had occurred, and two school staff members had to be treated for smoke inhalation.

Under the terms of a court decision, Evan had to take part in TAPP-C. For several weeks, Evan and his mother met with a counsellor and a fire service educator. Neither Evan nor his mother wanted to set quitting smoking as a treatment goal. They were, however, willing to work together to come up with rules to guide where and when Evan would be allowed to smoke. They also came up with strategies to limit Evan's access to matches and cigarette lighters at home and in the community. Evan worked on ways to control his desire to play with fire and to control his temper. He thought about safer activities that he could enjoy doing instead of playing with fire, such as playing sports. He realized that by being good at certain sports, he could also win the approval of his friends. One year after the treatment ended, Evan had set no other fires and was still working on not losing his temper.

Interventions that target environmental risk and protective factors

Mentoring programs

Mentoring programs, such as Big Brothers and Big Sisters, involve matching a young person with a nurturing adult. The pair meets regularly to take part in extracurricular activities suited to the young person's age and interests, such as going to movies or the library, or playing or watching sports. Mentors can act as friends, advocates and positive role models. They can talk to the child or youth with whom they are matched to find out about the young person's life, problems and desires, and to provide support, approval and respect. Young people's relationships with their mentors can add to their parents' support, or in some cases replace it (if, for example, parents are absent or uninvolved).

As noted in Chapter 3, having a solid relationship with at least one empathetic adult is a protective factor against aggression. A study of the Big Brothers and Big Sisters program showed that among young people aged 10 to 16 who participated in the program, boys had half the rate of drug use, girls had half the rate of truancy (skipping school), and both groups hit other people substantially less often than their counterparts of the same age who were waiting to be teamed up with a mentor. Young people already in the program were also more confident about school, got along better with their families, and reported fewer feelings of anger, fear, frustration or worry.

Children who are matched up with nurturing adults in mentoring programs are most often preadolescents from single-parent families. However, sometimes adolescents, as well as children from two-parent families, take part in such programs. Before being accepted into a mentoring program, young people must undergo an assessment to determine if they are likely to benefit. Some—for example, those who have experienced a history of abuse—may not possess enough trust to enter into a successful emotional relationship with a mentor.

Youth workers

Youth workers are mostly young adults interested in direct service who have graduated from community college programs. They are employed in a wide variety of settings, including schools, community centres, drop-in centres and youth homes. They are sometimes also employed by social service agencies to work directly on the streets. Youth workers often share the culture of those they work among and have had some similar life experiences; they may dress like the youth they work with and "talk the same language." In any setting, youth workers are therefore often the most "in the know" concerning what is really going on in the lives of their clients. They will frequently be the first to be tipped off if a young person has been dealing drugs, has been beaten up or has experienced sexual assault.

Youth workers serve as mentors who can influence young people in positive ways and intervene when they are in trouble. They can be in the best position to persuade youth not to join gangs, and to help those who are in gangs find a way out. They can help young people realize that they possess a range of skills and strengths that will allow them to achieve success through socially acceptable and legitimate means. Youth workers can also serve as important intermediaries between young people and social workers, psychologists and other health care providers.

School and classroom intervention programs

Schools that have programs to promote positive behaviours and a sense of student attachment have fewer incidents involving aggression and other conduct problems. The components of such programs generally include:
• clear-cut rules and procedures
• routines for communicating expectations
• adequate supervision and monitoring of students
• fair and consistent consequences for students who break the rules
• rewards for positive behaviours.

Other school interventions for aggression can include bullying prevention programs and after-school activity programs. *(For information on bullying prevention programs, see Chapter 2.)*

Classroom interventions for aggression can include human relations education programs (which foster an appreciation of people of different socio-cultural backgrounds), as well as programs that teach social skills, conflict resolution and decision-making skills.

After-school programs and activities

Many incidents involving aggressive behaviours among young people occur in the hours after school. Extracurricular activities help reduce the incidence of aggressive behaviour by children and adolescents in two ways: they provide young people with opportunities to develop positive personal and social skills, and they consume leisure hours so that young people have less unsupervised time in which to engage in aggressive and other anti-social behaviours, including social aggression *(discussed in Chapter 2).*

A range of organizations—such as community agencies, YMCAs and YWCAs, parks and recreation departments, and religious organizations—offer after-school programs of many kinds at varying prices, including some that are free.

Interventions that target individual, family and environmental risk and protective factors together

Multi-systemic therapy

Some researchers believe that the best way to reduce aggressive behaviour among young people, especially when it is extreme, is through the use of a variety of approaches that together target as many risk and protective factors as possible. Multi-systemic therapy (MST) involves young people, their families and their communities. It is an intensive treatment that incorporates a combination of some or all of the interventions already mentioned in this chapter. Researchers in the United States have recommended MST to tackle the problems of youth gangs in cities such as Los Angeles. This approach demands substantial funding and co-operation among different agencies.

Prevention and early intervention programs

Researchers on aggression have found that the earlier a young person with problem aggression is identified and treated, the greater the chance that the chosen treatment will have lasting benefits. It's not surprising, then, that they have developed interventions designed to stop the development of aggressive behaviour before any serious problems emerge. Such prevention and early intervention programs focus on helping young people who are starting to show behavioural problems, or who are at risk of developing such problems in the future because of the presence of certain risk factors in their lives.

These programs can be aimed at individuals, at families or at whole communities. Like MST, they can involve any combination of the interventions discussed in this chapter. They can be delivered to individuals or groups in a wide variety of settings. Building a drop-in recreational centre for young people in a socially disadvantaged neighbourhood is one example of a prevention and early intervention program targeted at helping a community at risk.

One effective prevention and early intervention program aimed at helping young children is a 12-week program called The Incredible Years. Developed by Dr. Carolyn Webster Stratton in Seattle, Washington, it is now offered across North America by a variety of agencies, as well as at some schools. Its goal is to help children aged about two to eight years who are starting to show behavioural problems. Making use of interactive videos, The Incredible Years focuses on changing the way parents and teachers treat children and youth. Parents are taught effective ways to communicate with and manage their children, as well as ways to cope with conflicts. They are also taught strategies to manage their own anger and stress, and to strengthen their social supports. Teachers are taught how to strengthen relationships with students, effectively discipline their classes, and increase collaboration with parents. They are also shown methods for teaching social skills and anger management as part of their day-to-day lessons. A number of studies have shown that The Incredible Years works to reduce and prevent behaviour problems among the children of participating parents.

Universal prevention programs

A universal prevention program is an intervention that is delivered broadly, to as many people as possible—not just to those people who have been identified as either having, or being at risk for developing, a problem.

One successful example of a universal prevention program for aggression is Roots of Empathy, developed in 1996 by Mary Gordon, an award-winning teacher, child advocate and parenting expert. Roots of Empathy has been implemented in thousands of elementary- and middle-school classes, from kindergarten to Grade 8, in nine provinces across Canada. As its name suggests, the program focuses on raising levels of empathy among young children.

The heart of Roots of Empathy is simple, thoughtful and imaginative: Every three weeks over the course of a school year, a baby and parent visit a classroom.

During the visits, students have an opportunity to play, interact and bond with the baby. With the help of an instructor, who accompanies the baby and parent on their classroom visits, students learn about the baby's needs, personality, and mental and physical growth. During visits, younger children will, for example, watch the baby enjoy looking at a picture book that they have made. Older children will learn about the causes of Sudden Infant Death Syndrome and how to prevent it. Roots of Empathy has been shown in Canadian studies to increase knowledge of emotions and positive social behaviours and to decrease incidents of aggression among program participants.

Universal prevention programs, such as Roots of Empathy, are most often designed to reach younger children in order to stop the development of harmful and anti-social behaviours before they have started. Such broadly targeted programs could help children whose problems with aggression are not clearly evident or who might be overlooked because their risk factors have not been identified. They are also worthy because, in their delivery, no children are singled out as "problems" or "potential problems."

SHANA'S STORY
How Shana was helped

In Chapter 3, we met seven-year-old Shana, who often pushed or hit other children in her class, was verbally aggressive with her teachers, and frequently scratched her mother. On the advice of Shana's teacher, her mother took her daughter to be assessed by a child psychiatrist.

During the assessment, the psychiatrist discovered that Shana had several risk factors for aggression: She had been born to a teenaged mother who did not provide Shana with consistent care, warmth and support. Instead, Shana's mother broke promises to her and threatened her with abandonment and foster care. Her mother also used drugs, worked as a prostitute and exposed her to adult problems. The psychiatrist diagnosed Shana as having oppositional defiant disorder (ODD), another risk factor for aggression. Shana did, however, have a high IQ, which is a protective factor.

The psychiatrist considered these factors and came up with a treatment plan for Shana that combined various approaches. He recommended that she be enrolled in an intervention program offered at her school that combined cognitive-behavioural therapy with special education. He also suggested that Shana's mother see a counsellor to help her learn to interact with her daughter in a more loving, nurturing way, as well as to face the problems in her own life.

To help Shana, staff of the school program used many of the known methods for working with young people with ODD (see Chapter 8). For example, they gave Shana simple tasks (such as handing out folders to other students) that made her feel helpful, and then rewarded her with praise after she had completed them.

The staff felt that Shana also needed some clearly set limits: When she refused to do a task, she was given options and told what would happen if she didn't comply. When she was rude or aggressive, staff told her they were not pleased with her behaviour; they stressed, however, that they still cared about her. They encouraged Shana to find an adult to talk to about her problems and feelings, since they recognized that her mother wasn't providing her with needed care and support. They also taught Shana communication and social skills, and anger management skills to help her change her aggressive behaviours. Over the course of the five-month program, Shana's behaviour began to improve. Shana eventually went back to study in a regular classroom and later entered an enriched academic program.

Upon the advice of Shana's psychiatrist, her mother, Charmaine, eventually agreed to attend family therapy sessions with Shana, as well as seeing her individual counsellor. Working with a counsellor, Charmaine slowly began to change her own behaviour. She stopped using drugs and quit prostitution. She enrolled in a beauty school and, after her training, found work as a hairdresser.

Chapter 8

Diagnosis

As mentioned in Chapter 6, during the course of an assessment, a health care provider may sometimes make a diagnosis—that is, determine that a young person has a mental health disorder identified in the *Diagnostic and Statistical Manual of Mental Disorders* (DSM). To say that someone meets the criteria for a diagnosis, the person making the assessment must be convinced that a young person has displayed a certain set of behaviours, or symptoms, for a certain amount of time, as outlined in the DSM. He or she must also be convinced that these behaviours prevent the young person from functioning normally at home, at school or in relationships with peers and others. Only a medical doctor, a psychiatrist or a psychologist can make a diagnosis. Other health care providers, such as nurses or social workers, can do assessments, but are not qualified to diagnose mental health disorders.

As noted elsewhere in this book, a number of mental health disorders are often associated with aggression problems among young people. (Not all young people who behave aggressively, however, have a mental health disorder.) On the following pages you will find a discussion of each of these disorders and its symptoms as described in the DSM. Some young people have more than one disorder, a situation that can complicate diagnosis and treatment.

Pros and cons of a diagnosis

Health care providers who are qualified to make diagnoses have special training in standardized methods for understanding young people's behaviour. Diagnoses make it possible to compare and contrast young people who are of the same age and developmental level. They also allow health care providers to apply what they have learned from treating one group of young people in order to help others more quickly and effectively.

If, as is often the case, a young person receives treatment from more than one health care provider at the same time, a diagnosis ensures that all these providers are working together. This collaboration enables them to understand the totality of the young person's behaviour and circumstances, and thus to provide him or her with the most effective treatment.

The goal of a diagnosis is not to place a young person into a slot. Some parents may worry, however, that a diagnosis will do exactly that—place a harmful label on their child. These worries are sometimes justified: sometimes the adults working with a young person who has been given a diagnosis lose their focus on that individual's unique personality and needs. They may no longer see the whole person, but only the disorder—and they might make incorrect assumptions.

Unfortunately, there is a stigma (negative attitudes and negative behaviour) attached to mental health disorders. Young people who have been diagnosed with a disorder may find themselves facing prejudice and discrimination. For example, they may find that they are refused entrance to a private school or summer camp.

If you work with young people, you can avoid labelling them by carefully choosing the language you use, and by not focusing on the disorder during your day-to-day interactions with the young person or during conversations with others. For example, instead of speaking about a boy's conduct disorder, you might say, "He has some problems controlling his anger and frustration, and we are working together to resolve those problems." Instead of referring to an "aggressive child," you might speak about "a child who is behaving aggressively and who is working toward changing her behaviour in future."

Disruptive behaviour disorders

Disruptive behaviour disorders are frequently diagnosed in children or adolescents who have been referred to mental health centres or youth justice settings. Three of the most common such disorders (oppositional defiant disorder, attention-deficit/hyperactivity disorder and conduct disorder) are discussed on the following pages.

Oppositional defiant disorder

All young people are *oppositional* (verbally contrary or defiant) from time to time, particularly when they are tired, hungry or emotionally upset. They may argue or talk back, and may disobey parents, teachers and other adults. Oppositional behaviour is most frequently observed among two- to three-year-olds and early adolescents.

Some young people are more oppositional than the average young person. Young people may be diagnosed with oppositional defiant disorder (ODD) when:
• their unco-operative and hostile behaviour is so frequent and consistent that it makes them stand out from other children or youth who are of the same age and developmental level, *and*
• it affects their family, social and school life.

The causes of ODD are unknown, but both genetic and environmental factors may play a role. ODD has some symptoms that overlap with conduct disorder, described below. It tends to be diagnosed in younger children, usually those who are younger than eight. Some children who are diagnosed with ODD are later diagnosed with conduct disorder. A young person who shows symptoms of aggression that are more severe than those associated with ODD may be diagnosed with conduct disorder from the start. ODD often occurs along with attention-deficit/hyperactivity disorder.

Studies have shown different rates of ODD among young people, ranging from two per cent to 16 per cent.

Symptoms of ODD

ODD may be diagnosed in young people if they display negative, hostile and defiant behaviour that lasts for six months or more, with four or more of the following symptoms present:
• excessive arguing with adults
• active defiance and refusal to comply with adult requests and rules
• repeated attempts to annoy or upset people
• often blaming others for their own mistakes or misbehaviour
• often acting touchy or easily annoyed by others
• frequent loss of temper
• frequent feelings of anger and resentment
• often acting spiteful or vindictive*

---

*Adapted with permission from the *Diagnostic and Statistical Manual of Mental Disorders,* Fourth Edition, Text Revision. Copyright 2000, American Psychiatric Association.

Managing ODD

You may come into contact with young people who you know have (or might have) ODD. Here are some simple techniques to encourage them to behave in more socially acceptable ways:
- Always build on the positives. Give young people praise and positive reinforcement whenever they show flexibility or co-operation.
- Don't have too many rules, but focus on a few important ones, such as those that involve safety.
- Instead of using direct commands, stay more neutral. For example, say, "We need to tidy up before we go outside" instead of "Tidy up." When dealing with older children and adolescents, consider making requests for them to do chores or activities in writing rather than giving verbal commands.
- If you are in the middle of a conflict with a young person who has ODD, pause for a moment—especially if you think the conflict is getting worse rather than being resolved. You might say, for example, "It seems that we are not understanding each other clearly. We are just getting angrier. Let's count to 10 and take a few deep breaths." By taking a break from an argument, you model a method the young person can use to gain self-control and prevent overreacting to a situation. When you see young people using this "time out" technique themselves, support them with praise.
- Pick your conflicts. Since young people with ODD have trouble avoiding power struggles, prioritize the things you want them to do.
- Set up reasonable, age-appropriate limits with consequences that can be enforced consistently.

Effective treatment programs, or interventions, for young people with ODD include:
- cognitive-behavioural therapy to decrease negativity
- anger management training to help with temper control
- parent management skills training programs to help parents learn to manage their children's behaviour.

(For a discussion of these and other interventions, see Chapter 7.)

Attention-deficit/hyperactivity disorder

Attention-deficit/hyperactivity disorder (ADHD) is one of the most common disorders among young people. Although aggression is not specifically a symptom of ADHD, the disorder is often diagnosed in young people who behave aggressively.

ADHD affects young people's attention span and concentration. It can also affect how impulsive and active they are. Most young people are, at times, inattentive, distractible, impulsive or highly active. A young person may be diagnosed with ADHD when such behaviours occur more frequently and are more severe than is considered average among young people of the same age or developmental level.

A diagnosis of ADHD might also result if the behaviours persist over time and negatively affect a young person's family and his or her social and school life.

Studies have not shown exactly how ADHD and aggression in young people are linked. Some behaviours that are not clearly defined symptoms of ADHD, but have been shown to be associated with it, may lead to aggression. They include:
• low tolerance for frustration
• temper outbursts
• emotional instability
• stubbornness
• conflicts with parents
• problems with social skills
• low self-esteem.

Studies have shown different rates of ADHD among young people, ranging from one per cent to 13 per cent. ADHD is three to four times more common in boys than girls.

Symptoms of ADHD

The symptoms of ADHD fall into two main groups: inattentive behaviours; and hyperactive and impulsive behaviours. Young people may be diagnosed with ADHD if, for the past six months or more, they have displayed six or more symptoms of either (a) inattentive behaviours or (b) hyperactive or impulsive behaviours.

(a) INATTENTIVE BEHAVIOURS
• often doesn't pay attention to details or makes what appear to be careless mistakes in schoolwork or other activities
• usually has problems keeping focused on work or activities
• often doesn't seem to listen when spoken to
• frequently doesn't follow through on instructions and doesn't finish tasks
• often has difficulty organizing tasks
• usually doesn't like to do tasks that call for ongoing thinking
• often loses things
• is often easily distracted
• often forgets things

(b) HYPERACTIVE BEHAVIOURS
• often fidgets and squirms in chair
• often leaves seat when required to sit still
• frequently runs or climbs excessively (or, for adolescents, feels restless)
• often talks excessively
• usually has difficulty playing quietly
• is constantly in motion

IMPULSIVE BEHAVIOURS
• usually has problems waiting for a turn
• regularly blurts out answers before questions have been completed
• often interrupts or intrudes on others' conversations or games*

---

*Adapted with permission from the *Diagnostic and Statistical Manual of Mental Disorders*, Fourth Edition, Text Revision. Copyright 2000, American Psychiatric Association.

Managing ADHD

A number of treatment interventions are effective in helping young people with ADHD. Cognitive-behavioural therapy can help build their self-esteem, reduce negative thoughts and improve their problem-solving skills; it can also help them learn self-control and improve their social skills. Parents of young people with ADHD can learn how to better manage their children's behaviour by taking parent management skills training. Educators can design programs for young people with ADHD to encourage success rather than failure—and to address any coexisting learning disabilities that they might have, such as difficulty with reading. A child who is diagnosed with ADHD and treated appropriately can have a productive and successful life. *(For a discussion of common interventions, see Chapter 7.)*

If you work or volunteer with young people who have (or who you think might have) ADHD, you may find the following tips helpful:
• Provide the young person with as structured an environment and as predictable a routine as possible.
• Clearly warn of any changes in routine in advance.
• Provide a calm, quiet atmosphere without too many visual distractions.
• Begin conversations by addressing the young person directly, using eye contact; wait until he or she is paying attention before speaking.
• Give instructions one step at a time, rather than issuing multiple requests at once. Have the young person repeat the instructions back to you.
• Provide clear and simple rules; consider posting them somewhere visible.
• Find out what the young person is good at and incorporate this into activities.
• Ask the young person what he or she thinks will help.

In a classroom setting:
• Provide short work periods.
• Break down assignments into small, manageable units.
• Seat the student at the front of the class and away from distractions.
• Give extra time for tests, and hand out one sheet of a multi-page test at a time.
• Communicate each homework assignment a number of times, both verbally and in writing.
• Have the student use a daily planner to keep a record of what he or she has done and still needs to do.
• Encourage the student to use aids to deal with symptoms, such as earplugs to avoid distractions or a stress ball to play with instead of fidgeting.
• For a younger child, assign simple errands, so that he or she can move around and feel useful.

Conduct disorder

Conduct disorder (CD) may be diagnosed in a child or adolescent who has repeatedly and consistently shown a number of severely aggressive and anti-social behaviours. Young people with CD find it very difficult to follow rules and behave in socially acceptable ways. They are often viewed by parents, teachers, social service providers, other adults and their peers as "bad" rather than as having a mental health problem.

Many factors may contribute to a young person developing CD, including brain damage, genetic makeup, failure at school and traumatic life experiences, such as abuse. Young people with CD may also have other mental health disorders.

The DSM makes a distinction between young people who display at least one symptom of the disorder before the age of 10 and those who first display symptoms of the disorder after the age of 10. Those in the former group are more likely than those in the latter group to continue to display severely aggressive, anti-social and illegal behaviour over time. They are also more likely to be boys, whereas young people in the latter group are as likely to be girls as boys.

Studies have shown different rates of CD among young people, varying from one per cent to nine per cent.

Symptoms of CD

Young people may be diagnosed with conduct disorder if they have displayed three or more of the following symptoms in the past 12 months, with at least one symptom also present in the past six months:

AGGRESSION TOWARD PEOPLE AND ANIMALS
• frequently bullies, threatens or intimidates others
• often initiates physical fights
• has used a weapon that could cause serious physical harm to others
  (for example, a bat, brick, broken bottle, knife or gun)
• has been physically cruel to people
• has been physically cruel to animals
• has stolen from victims while confronting them (for example, during an assault)
• has forced someone into sexual activity

DESTRUCTION OF PROPERTY
• has deliberately engaged in fire setting with the intention of causing damage
• has deliberately destroyed others' property

DECEITFULNESS OR STEALING
• has broken into someone else's building, house or car
• often lies to obtain goods or favours, or to avoid obligations
• has stolen valuable items without confronting a victim (for example, shoplifting, but without breaking and entering)

SERIOUS VIOLATIONS OF RULES
- often stays out at night despite parental objections (starting before age 13)
- has run away from home overnight at least twice
- is often truant from school (starting before age 13)*

Managing CD

Studies indicate that the most effective way to manage CD among young people is through the use of a varied approach that involves a wide range of programs, including training in social skills, problem-solving skills, anger management and (for the parents) parent management skills training. Providing such treatment often requires co-ordination among people working in various systems: the education system, the mental health system, the child welfare system and, in the case of a young person in trouble with the law, the juvenile justice system. Young people with conduct disorder can, however, be difficult to engage in treatment programs for various reasons. They may, for example, have poor verbal skills or low intelligence. The earlier and younger a child with conduct disorder receives treatment, the more likely it is that the treatment will show benefits.

LUCAS'S STORY
Helping a boy with ADHD and ODD

Lucas and his older brother were raised by a single mother. His mother adored his brother, but had admitted to Lucas that she did not like him.

Lucas's behaviour was difficult to manage. By the age of six, he often made lewd gestures and comments that were sexually provocative or insulting. He deliberately tried to embarrass people, remarking, for example, on his teacher's breast size. When asked to do his schoolwork, he would show an outburst of temper and use crude language.

Upon the recommendation of his teacher, his mother took him to see a child psychiatrist. Because of his sexual knowledge, the psychiatrist at first thought that Lucas might have been sexually abused or exposed to sexual behaviour. After completing his assessment, however, the psychiatrist concluded that Lucas had picked up his sexual language and gestures from older children; he had learned that, by using them, he could attract adult attention and avoid doing his schoolwork. The psychiatrist also diagnosed Lucas as having attention-deficit/hyperactivity disorder (ADHD) and oppositional defiant disorder (ODD). He recommended that Lucas take medication to help control the symptoms of his disorders, but his mother initially refused.

*Adapted with permission from the *Diagnostic and Statistical Manual of Mental Disorders*, Fourth Edition, Text Revision. Copyright 2000, American Psychiatric Association.

Lucas's treatment plan

Lucas was placed in a special needs class taught by a special education teacher, who was assisted by a support staff of counsellors. The staff gave Lucas a lot of positive attention, complimenting him when he did his work. At first, Lucas continued to mock and ridicule them. Staff dealt with his insults and sexual language by not reacting emotionally. They calmly told him that those words should not be used in class. Staff also brought in a nurse to educate the class about the body. Lucas was surprised to hear an adult coolly discussing body parts that he often mentioned during his outbursts.

After each of his outbursts, staff would approach Lucas and calmly tell him that they thought he might be trying to get their attention. They would ask him what he wanted or what he was really trying to say. They also used anger management training techniques *(discussed in Chapter 7)* to slowly teach Lucas that, while anger is a common human emotion, he needed to find more socially acceptable ways to express his feelings of frustration.

Lucas's teacher and counsellors repeatedly showed him that, while they did not approve of his behaviour, they accepted him completely as a person. In this way, they slowly built up a relationship with him—one in which he trusted them and felt safe. The relationships that Lucas developed with the staff of his special education class helped raise his self-esteem.

Lucas gradually stopped using rude and sexually provocative words. However, sometimes he still refused to do his schoolwork. On these occasions, the staff would notice his eyes welling up with tears. They recognized that this behaviour was less severe and disruptive than his outbursts of temper had been—and that Lucas had achieved a great deal of success in terms of his self-control. Rather than punishing him for not working, they presented him with options: they suggested that they do the work together, or that Lucas ask a friend to help him. The staff also empathized with his struggle, pointing out times when they, too, felt nervous because their work was hard. Lucas gradually began to talk about his feelings when he was having trouble with his schoolwork.

The staff at Lucas's school took a varied approach, working with both Lucas and his mother at the same time. They patiently explained to her what they believed to be the causes of Lucas's behaviour: his low tolerance for frustration, poor self-esteem and poor social and communication skills. They also explained how ADHD and ODD were affecting his behaviour. Last but not least, they drew on their knowledge of parent management skills training programs *(see Chapter 7)*, encouraging Lucas's mother to become more involved in her son's life and to focus on his positive efforts rather than on her feelings of dislike. They also encouraged her to find strategies to cope and relax when she felt worn out by Lucas's behaviour. They empathized with her, pointing out that, at school, Lucas had a whole team of people who could take turns working with him, while at home she was the only adult present to face this challenge.

Lucas's mother agreed to put her son on medication for a trial period and noticed a difference in his behaviour. She also agreed to read to him every night, but she found this task too difficult. Instead, she tried to sit with him at a table while he drew pictures and to give him one compliment about his artwork. Gradually, she was able to spend more time with him doing different activities and to build up her relationship with him. As Lucas's behaviour improved, his mother started to see his strengths and understand and accept the ways in which he differed from other children. She recognized that challenges still lay ahead, but she was much more optimistic about her relationship with her son. Lucas's behaviour continued to improve at school and at home.

Substance use disorders

As noted in Chapter 3, substance use is a risk factor for aggression among young people. Substance use disorders (SUDs) include the abuse of, or dependence on, substances such as alcohol, medications or illegal drugs.

Experimenting with substances may begin among children as young as seven or eight. Many teenagers try substances, most commonly alcohol, cigarettes and cannabis. A 2005 study conducted by the Centre for Addiction and Mental Health of 7,726 Ontario students in grades 7 to 12 showed that 62 per cent had used alcohol in the past year, 23 per cent had engaged in binge drinking and 27 per cent had used cannabis.

The relationship between aggression and substance use is complicated. Due to their chemical makeup, the use of some substances, such as alcohol or cocaine, can increase the likelihood of aggressive behaviour; however, the use of other substances, such as cannabis or opioids (for example, heroin, OxyContin), can decrease the likelihood of aggressive behaviour.

The chemical effect of some substances can also lead more indirectly to aggressive behaviour. For example, the use of alcohol can reduce inhibitions and self-restraint, which can, in turn, increase the likelihood of impulsive behaviour. In young people who drink, this increased impulsiveness can then increase the likelihood that they will behave aggressively. In addition, the use of some substances can interfere with young people's ability to correctly read social signals. It can lead them to wrongly assume that others around them are hostile or unfriendly. Young people who misread social signals in this way are more likely to behave aggressively than those who do not.

Substance use can also put young people into situations that they would not otherwise find themselves in—situations that can increase the likelihood that they will behave aggressively. For example, while buying drugs illegally they might get into a physical fight, especially if they feel threatened or suspect that they have been cheated.

Young people may also behave aggressively when they are withdrawing from the use of a substance—especially if they have been using the substance in order to control aggressive impulses, negative emotions or angry feelings. Young people sometimes use substances in this way to "self-medicate" diagnosed or undiagnosed mental health problems and disorders.

A young person does not have to use substances consistently to experience harms from their use: a teen could binge drink on only one occasion, yet get alcohol poisoning or engage in violent or illegal behaviour.

Substance use may or may not directly affect a young person's problems with aggression. If left unchecked, however, it may interfere with interventions aimed at addressing aggression (or other problems).

Although many teens try substances, only a small fraction develop a substance use disorder. The risk is higher among those with emotional or behavioural problems. The DSM presents guidelines, summarized below, that health care providers can use to help diagnose substance abuse and substance dependence.

When looking over these guidelines, remember that young people often use substances in ways that do not meet the DSM's criteria for diagnosing an SUD. Many youth, for example, have a higher tolerance of substances than adults and undergo fewer symptoms when they withdraw. But even if their behaviour does not meet the criteria for a diagnosable SUD, young people can need specialized intervention in order to reduce the harms caused by substance use. *(See the section on managing substance use later in this chapter.)* Indeed, health care providers always need to find out whether the young people in their care are using substances. Substance use can contribute to or be related to a range of problem behaviours. It can also trigger, heighten, mask or mimic symptoms, or interact negatively with prescribed medication.

Symptoms of SUDs

Substance abuse refers to an unhealthy pattern of substance use indicated by the occurrence of one or more of the following symptoms within a 12-month period:
- repeated substance use resulting in a failure to fulfil roles at school, work or home
- repeated legal problems resulting from substance use, such as arrests for substance-related disorderly conduct

- repeated substance use in situations in which it is physically hazardous, such as while driving a car
- continued use despite the experience of family, social, school or work problems caused by, or aggravated by, the use of the substance.

Substance dependence refers to an unhealthy pattern of use indicated by the occurrence of three or more of the following symptoms within a 12-month period:
- the development of tolerance (needing more of the substance to get the desired effect, or finding that using the same amount of substance leads to a reduced effect)
- the appearance of withdrawal symptoms when the substance is no longer taken, or a need to keep taking the substance to ease or prevent withdrawal symptoms
- taking more of the substance or taking it for a longer period than originally intended
- having an ongoing desire, or making unsuccessful attempts, to cut down on substance use
- spending a lot of time trying to get the substance, using it or recovering from its effects
- giving up or cutting down on normal social, work, school or leisure activities
- continuing using the substance despite knowing that it is causing problems at home, with friends, at school or at work. *

Young people who start to show aggression problems earlier in life are more likely to develop an SUD than those whose aggression problems appear later. Many of those in the former group use substances to manage their behaviour and feelings, as an excuse for their behaviour or to enhance their feelings of power. Their use may also be the result of their being drawn into, and feeling comfortable with, a peer group that engages in various kinds of aggressive behaviours and substance use.

SUDs often occur with other disorders. For boys, SUDs often occur with CD and ADHD. For girls, SUDs are more likely to occur with major depressive disorder and bipolar disorder *(both discussed later in this chapter)*. SUDs also often occur among young people (particularly girls) who have experienced childhood sexual and physical abuse.

Managing substance use

In the past, interventions often focused on trying to get young people to completely stop their use of all substances. An alternative approach is *harm reduction*, a relatively recent development in substance use treatment, which

---

*Adapted with permission from the *Diagnostic and Statistical Manual of Mental Disorders*, Fourth Edition, Text Revision. Copyright 2000, American Psychiatric Association.

focuses on minimizing the consequences associated with substance use and other high-risk behaviours. With a harm-reduction approach, the main goal for the treatment of youth is lessening the harm caused by their substance use—which can, depending on the circumstances, involve helping them work toward reducing or stopping their use. For youth who are using a combination of substances (as they often are), the treatment might involve providing information about the effects of these substances, helping the young people make informed choices about their use and, if they are in agreement, helping them reduce their use of one or more of the substances, while at the same time stopping the use of one or more of the other substances that are causing them the most harm.

Most substance use treatment for youth is *psychosocial* in nature (for example, counselling); few cases involve medical intervention. When treating young people, substance use counsellors encourage them to keep participating as much as possible in their day-to-day activities, such as school—as well as to gradually build up extracurricular interests and activities. In sessions with youth (and sometimes their families), counsellors use various approaches to help motivate them to choose to make changes in their substance-use behaviours. One common approach is to help the young person understand what functions his or her substance use serves—for example, helping the person to manage social situations, or to cope with anger or frustration. The counsellor then helps the young person to build social, coping and other skills so that he or she does not feel the need to rely upon substances. Treatment identifies and builds on the young person's strengths.

The treatment continuum ranges from outpatient programs to residential care. Young people may also join self-help groups, such as Alcoholics Anonymous or Narcotics Anonymous, although they are often more comfortable and willing to attend group-based treatment with peers their own age. The treatment of youth who have more severe substance use problems may occasionally involve stays in public (hospital-based) or private substance use treatment centres, or treatment as outpatients of such centres. Some young people may stay in a group home or therapeutic community.

Treatment programs for young people with SUDs are designed to address not only the substance use itself, but also other behavioural problems that may be associated directly or indirectly with the use.

MARCO'S STORY
Helping a teen with substance dependence

Marco was raised in a traditional Portuguese-Canadian family in a tightly knit Portuguese urban neighbourhood. Growing up, Marco never did well in school; he just managed to get by. He spent a lot of time hanging out in the streets with other neighbourhood boys, sometimes getting into fights. His parents were not concerned about his behaviour, shrugging it off as normal boyish antics.

After Marco started high school, his behaviour became more socially unacceptable. He started getting into serious fights and using crack cocaine. He eventually stopped going to school, spending his time in bars with older teenaged boys instead. He liked to be seen as a tough guy.

Marco was charged with assault and drug possession several times. Many of the assault charges were related to drug deals. He also stole from his parents' home to buy crack, and threatened to hurt his father. His father kicked him out of the house several times, and he would go to live at his older brother's place. His mother always let him come back home.

Under the terms of the probation that resulted from the assault charges, Marco had to follow certain rules and conditions, such as a curfew. However, he was lax about doing so. His mother didn't set limits to help him follow the rules. His father acted as if he was completely uninterested in him. One day Marco stole from his brother. At that point, Marco's brother stopped being sympathetic toward him.

Marco's treatment plan

Under the terms of his probation—and because his brother insisted—Marco agreed to see a substance use counsellor for his crack use. The counsellor worked with Marco, using primarily a cognitive-behavioural therapy approach. *(For a discussion of this type of therapy, see Chapter 7.)* She helped him begin thinking about the life he wanted to lead, and how his crack use was not helping him do this.

In working with Marco, she also took a harm-reduction approach: she did not try to force Marco to stop using the drug. Instead, she helped him to become aware of the harms caused by his use of crack, and then to find ways to begin minimizing these harms. The counsellor took this approach because she felt that if Marco tried to suddenly quit using crack, he most likely would fail. She also recognized that Marco needed to find his own motivations to want to quit, which had not yet occurred when he first started therapy. And an initial failure might have discouraged him from continuing to make the effort to try to change his behaviour.

Besides helping Marco find ways to begin minimizing the harms caused by his crack use, the counsellor also helped him set realistic goals for himself. As Marco began working toward these goals, he became motivated to make changes in his crack use. He realized that he would not be able to attain his goals if he continued to use crack.

Through therapy, Marco gradually learned to understand what triggered his crack use. He also learned ways to avoid these triggers. Over time he managed to reduce his crack use and ultimately achieved abstinence.

In treating Marco, the counsellor took a varied approach and also involved Marco's family in therapy. *(For a discussion of family therapy, see Chapter 7.)* She wanted to help the family learn how to best support Marco in his struggle to change his behaviours and to help him see his family as caring and helpful. At first, Marco's brother came to sessions with him. Then his mother started coming. Eventually, Marco's father agreed to come as well. At that session, the counsellor helped Marco and his family negotiate and set limits together regarding which of Marco's behaviours were acceptable when he was living in his parents' home. She also helped the family agree on a set of consequences if Marco did not follow the family's code of behaviour. The counsellor worked with the parents to help them understand the importance of following through consistently and co-operatively to enforce the limits and consequences they had all agreed on.

Engaging the whole family was a key part of Marco's treatment. In treatment sessions, the counsellor learned that the family's lack of consistent rules had been a source of conflict between Marco's mother and father—and had sent mixed messages to their son. Bringing his father into the treatment process was a breakthrough for the whole family. Marco realized that his father did care about him, but did not know how to show those feelings and respond effectively to Marco's behaviour. Not knowing how to best guide Marco had made his father feel inadequate, and so he had avoided his son. He had also felt afraid for his son's future. The counsellor helped the family find ways to communicate and work with each other to create a more structured yet accepting environment.

Mood, anxiety and psychotic disorders

As part of a diagnosis for a young person who is behaving aggressively, a health care provider will routinely try to determine if the child or youth has any other disorders. These other disorders may not be directly associated with aggression. Some of the most common are discussed below.

Major depressive disorder

Major depressive disorder is a type of mood disorder. The key symptoms include sadness, loss of interest or pleasure in activities, and feelings of worthlessness or guilt. People who have major depressive disorder are more than just unhappy. They feel abnormally sad, despairing and hopeless in a sustained way for more than two weeks.

Unlike adults, young people who experience major depressive disorder may also appear irritable, angry, defiant or hostile, and aggressive. This may be because they don't have the maturity to express themselves in words or control their feelings.

Up to 90 per cent of young people with major depressive disorder have at least one other mental health condition, and many have two (for example, ADHD, CD or an anxiety disorder).

Cognitive-behavioural therapy (CBT) is considered by many health care providers to be the best way to treat mood disorders. *(For a discussion of CBT, see Chapter 7.)*

Posttraumatic stress disorder

Posttraumatic stress disorder (PTSD) is a type of anxiety disorder that can develop after a person has experienced or seen a traumatic event, such as physical or sexual abuse, a life-threatening accident, violence in the family or neighbourhood, or war. Young people with PTSD may display aggression, hostility and irritability as a result. Preschool children may have severe temper tantrums.

As with mood disorders, many health care providers consider CBT to be the best treatment for PTSD.

Psychotic disorders

The main symptoms of psychotic disorders are delusions and hallucinations. *Delusions* are false beliefs that significantly reduce a person's ability to function. Young people with delusions may, for example, believe that others are out to get them. *Hallucinations* are false perceptions. Young people with hallucinations may see, hear, smell, taste or feel things that are not there (such as bugs crawling over them).

People with psychotic disorders do not usually behave aggressively. They may do so, however, if they have another co-occurring disorder, such as an SUD or CD. Young people with psychotic disorders may be more likely to behave aggressively if their delusions make them feel threatened.

Psychotic disorders often need to be treated with prescription medications.

Fetal alcohol spectrum disorder

Alcohol can damage the brain and body of a fetus. Fetal alcohol spectrum disorder (FASD) is a broad term describing birth defects and conditions in people whose mothers drank alcohol when they were pregnant. When speaking about

FASD, health care providers may use other terms to refer to specific effects and conditions resulting from a fetus's exposure to alcohol. These terms include:
• fetal alcohol syndrome (FAS)
• partial fetal alcohol syndrome (pFAS)
• alcohol-related neurodevelopmental disorder (ARND)
• alcohol-related birth defects (ARBD).

Symptoms of FASD

The physical symptoms of FAS can include a small head or body, distinct facial features and brain damage. The physical symptoms of ARBD can include heart defects, hearing difficulties, vision problems and joint problems.

Young people with FASD can experience a range of physical, mental, behavioural and learning problems, including:
• poor organizational skills
• poor concentration, attention and memory
• trouble speaking well
• trouble learning to read
• trouble adapting to change
• poor judgment and problem-solving skills
• socially inappropriate behaviours
• poor ability to control impulsive behaviours (acting without thinking)
• low tolerance for frustration
• low level of understanding
• poor ability to learn from experience.

These problems can vary in intensity and can affect those with the disorder throughout their lives. Some people may have just one or two problems; others may have many. The types of problems young people with FASD have can also change as they get older.

Aggression is not directly associated with FASD. Some of the problems that young people with FASD experience may, however, increase the chance that they will behave aggressively over the course of their lives. For example, those who lack the ability to understand that their behaviours could provoke negative consequences, or who lack the ability to learn from experience, may get into trouble with the law. Indeed, a high percentage of youth in the criminal justice system have been identified with FASD.

Managing FASD

While the abnormalities, disabilities and negative behaviours associated with FASD are permanent, some of them can be altered with early intervention programs. Such programs focus on young people who are just starting to show behavioural problems. Young people diagnosed with FASD can be managed so they don't have the opportunity to make poor choices. They can also be helped to develop socially acceptable behaviours and, above all, maintain their self-esteem. The best treatment programs for FASD use a variety of approaches.

Young people with FASD often benefit from a calm, highly structured environment and a consistent routine in which there are clear expectations that can be externally influenced and monitored. Treatments for young people with FASD most often do not involve instructing them to develop internal motivation and controls.

If you work or volunteer with young people who have (or who you think might have) FASD, the following ideas may help in your interactions with them:
• Begin conversations by addressing the young person directly.
• Always make eye contact, and wait until the young person is paying attention before speaking.
• Provide a calm, quiet atmosphere with limited visual distractions.
• Speak slowly and pause between sentences.
• Warn of any changes to routine in advance.
• When giving a set of instructions, give them one at a time and then repeat them.
• Don't use words or expressions that have more than one meaning.
• Make sure that the young person not only can repeat rules, but can also understand their meaning.
• Post notes in obvious places to remind the young person of the tasks that need to be done.

If you are teaching young people who have been diagnosed with FASD, you may also find it effective to reduce your academic expectations and stress the teaching of basic life skills—skills that will enable young people to look after themselves in the future. In some cases, young people with FASD may behave in ways that resemble the behaviour of those with ADHD, and you may find some of the treatment approaches used to help young people with ADHD to be useful.

Medical management of mental health disorders

Most young people who behave aggressively will never be prescribed medication (drugs) to control their behaviours. Medication is used less often in the treatment of mental health disorders and conditions in young people than in adults. This is because there is little research on the long-term effects of most drugs on growing children.

Doctors, however, may sometimes decide to prescribe medications to treat young people who behave aggressively and who have also been diagnosed with one or more of the mental health disorders discussed above. The goal of drug therapy is to reduce or manage severe behaviour symptoms that have not responded to other types of therapy.

Only medical doctors, such as child psychiatrists or pediatricians, can prescribe drugs for young people. Before prescribing any medications, a doctor will:
• make a diagnosis
• consider the young person's current symptoms and what treatments he or she has already undergone
• assess which medication(s) would be most appropriate, effective and safe for the person.

Some of the drugs that have been used successfully to treat aggression in CD and ODD include risperidone (Risperdal), lithium, valproate/valproic acid (Depakote) and methylphenidate (Ritalin). Methylphenidate is a widely prescribed stimulant that has proven effective in reducing the main symptoms of ADHD in more than 150 studies. These studies have consistently shown its effectiveness in reducing the intensity, frequency and duration of violent and aggressive episodes.

Young people who have mental health disorders are not usually treated with medications alone. Drug therapy is almost always accompanied by a selection of other, psychosocial treatments or interventions *(for a discussion of these interventions, see Chapter 7)*. The doctors prescribing drugs therefore become part of a broader treatment team. As part of a team, their task is to administer and manage the drug therapy. They monitor their young patients regularly to observe and chart the benefits and side-effects of all prescribed medications. They may sometimes decide to change the dose or schedule of a medication, or to wean a young person off a medication if its side-effects seem to be outweighing its benefits.

Afterword

As noted at the start of this book, aggression in young people is an important social issue. Children and youth who behave aggressively may harm not only themselves, but also their families, their communities and society at large. Fortunately, there are many early intervention and treatment programs that have been proven to help young people who show signs of aggression and significantly reduce these harmful outcomes.

There is, furthermore, evidence to show that the best way to deal with the social problem of young people and aggression is to prevent it from occurring in the first place. Prevention can be accomplished not only through the implementation of specifically targeted programs but also through the building of a society that reduces the relevant risk factors and enhances the protective factors.

Inherent in such an approach is the recognition that the levels of aggression—and overall mental health—found in young people is determined in part by a range of factors that are beyond their control. These social factors, or determinants of health, include the quality of housing, schools and neighbourhoods; they also include factors that reflect young people's (and their families') access to social services and opportunities, and the extent to which they can live, study and work safely in an equitable environment that is free of poverty, prejudice and discrimination.

Seeking to prevent and reduce aggression in young people through the general betterment of society falls under the broadly defined activity of health promotion. *Health promotion* involves improving the ability of people, and the families and communities they live in, to take control over their lives and improve their health.

If you work or volunteer with young people and you are concerned about the public health issue of aggression in children and youth, consider becoming more socially active in your own community. Here are some ways you can get involved:

- Organize a committee to help your local school set up a bullying prevention program *(see the section on bullying in Chapter 2)* as well as an after-school activities program. After-school programs need not cost a great deal; there may be parents in your community who have athletic, artistic or language skills and who are willing to devote a few hours a week to leading an activity.

- Write to your community's political representatives. Let them know that it is important to fund after-school activities. Also encourage them to fund free or low-cost programs aimed at helping parents improve their skills (such as parent training programs) and relieve stress (such as yoga classes).

- Lobby politicians to fund school psychologists, social workers, special-education teachers, guidance counsellors and youth workers. In many areas, the only health care providers and support workers that young people have the opportunity to see are those who work in their schools.

- Encourage the young people you know to get involved in community and volunteer work. Through such work, young people can learn to work co-operatively with others, practise decision-making and problem-solving skills, develop empathy, and enhance their social skills. Lobby local school boards to grant students the opportunity to participate in volunteer and community service activities for high school credit (if they are not already able to do so in your area).

- Older youth benefit from meaningful work opportunities. Lobby the owners of companies and businesses in your community to set up co-operative and apprenticeship programs. Workplaces can also be encouraged to donate used computers and other multimedia equipment to schools and organizations that serve youth; to sponsor events such as science fairs, contests and community dances; and to support young people's sports teams.

- Start a petition to have a good publicly funded recreation centre built in your neighbourhood.

- Media play a central role in the lives of children and youth. You can work to put pressure on the people who work in various media to:
    - portray young people engaging in leadership roles and healthy activities
    - involve children and youth, allowing them to publish or broadcast their views
    - sponsor youth sports and activities
    - provide coverage of local and national events involving young people
    - encourage creativity
    - restrict excessive portrayals of violence.

- Lobby neighbourhood, municipal, provincial and federal governments and associations—through letter-writing campaigns, e-mails and petitions—to adequately fund programs that will help support struggling young people and their families. Government and non-governmental agencies must all work together to build supportive environments with the aim of providing:
    - safe, affordable housing, schools and communities
    - nutritional programs in schools and in the community
    - high-quality day care and schools
    - skills training and job-creation programs for adults
    - adequate wages, employee benefits (such as time off work to raise children) and unemployment benefits
    - recognition of educational and professional qualifications obtained in other countries

- English-language training for young people and adults
- free (or reduced-fee) access to neighbourhood activities, such as sports, arts and other recreational opportunities
- easy one-stop resource centres to help parents find needed services.

Traditionally, communities have turned to law enforcement agencies and the juvenile justice system to address the social harm caused by aggression in young people. Research has shown that punishing young offenders is largely ineffective. Young people who have been sent away to reform institutions or jails eventually return to their families and communities. Unless their underlying behavioural problems have been treated successfully, they are likely to commit further acts of aggression.

Reducing risk factors and enhancing protective factors for aggression involves implementing healthy public policies and laws that bring about fairness of opportunity (such as universal access to education, health and social services); social justice (such as the elimination of poverty, prejudice and discrimination); and mutual respect for everyone's gender, culture, sexual orientation, religion and spirituality, and abilities.

It will take a good deal of time, will, energy and long-term commitment to address the problem of aggression in young people, and to build supportive environments in which all young people have an equal opportunity to thrive. There are already in place proven effective interventions—many of which have been discussed in this book—to help young people with aggression problems. The earlier these problems are identified and treated, the greater the chance that young people will behave in ways that will benefit, rather than harm, society.

Sources

Achenbach, T.M. & Rescorla, L.A. (2001). *Manual for the ASEBA School-Age Forms and Profiles.* Burlington, VT: University of Vermont, Research Center for Children, Youth & Families.

Adlaf, E. & Paglia-Boak, A. (2005). *Drug Use among Ontario Students 1977–2005: Detailed OSDUS Findings.* Toronto: Centre for Addiction and Mental Health.

American Academy of Child & Adolescent Psychiatry. *Facts for Families: Children with Oppositional Defiant Disorder.* Washington, DC: Author. Available: www.aacap.org. Accessed November 3, 2006.

American Psychiatric Association. (2000). *Diagnostic and Statistical Manual of Mental Disorders* (4th ed., text revision). Washington, DC: Author.

American Psychological Association. (2005). *Controlling Anger—Before It Controls You.* Washington, DC: Author. Available: www.apa.org/topics/controlanger.html. Accessed November 3, 2006.

Baillargeon, R., Tremblay, R.E. & Willms, J.D. (1999). *The Prevalence of Physical Aggression in Canadian Children: A Multi-Group Latent Class Analysis of Data from the First Collection Cycle (1994–1995) of the NLSCY.* Hull, QC: Human Resources Development Canada.

Baker, J.E. *Sticks and Stones Will Break My Bones, and Names Hurt Too.* Edison, NJ: Asperger Syndrome Education Network. Available: www.aspennj.org/baker.html. Accessed November 3, 2006.

Bassarath, L.E. (2001). *Youth Violence Prevention: A Guide for Concerned Parents and Professionals.* Lincoln, NE: Writers Club Press.

Bassarath, L.E. (2003). Medication strategies in childhood aggression: A review. *Canadian Journal of Psychiatry, 48* (6), 367–373.

Benson, B.A. (1995). Psychosocial interventions update: Problem solving skills training. *The Habilitative Mental Healthcare Newsletter, 14* (1).

Bjorkqvist, K., Lagerspetz, K.M.J. & Kaukiainen, A. (1992). Do girls manipulate and boys fight? Developmental trends in regard to direct and indirect aggression. *Aggressive Behavior, 18,* 117–127.

Bloomquist, M.L. & Schnell, S.V. (2002). *Helping Children with Aggression and Conduct Problems. Best Practices for Intervention.* New York: Guilford Press.

Bukstein, O.G. (2005, June). *Summary of the Practice Parameters for the Assessment and Treatment of Children and Adolescents with Substance Use Disorders. Practice Parameters, Volume 44.* Available: www.aacap.org. Accessed November 17, 2006.

Cairns, R.B. & Cairns, B.D. (1984). Predicting aggressive patterns in girls and boys: A developmental study. *Behaviour, 10,* 227–242.

Cairns, R.B., Cairns, B.D., Neckerman, H.J. & Ferguson, L.L. (1989). Growth and aggression: 1—Childhood to early adolescence. *Developmental Psychology, 25* (2), 320–330.

California Council on Criminal Justice. (1989). *State Task Force on Gangs and Drugs: Final Report.* Sacramento, CA: California Council on Criminal Justice.

Centre for Addiction and Mental Health. (2002). *Youth and Violence: What's the Story? Fast Facts & Topical Tips for Working with Youth.* Toronto: Author.

Centre for Addiction and Mental Health. (2003). *Challenges & Choices: Finding Mental Health Services in Ontario.* Toronto: Author.

Center for Mental Health in Schools at UCLA. (1999). *An Introductory Packet on Conduct and Behavior Problems: Intervention and Resources for School Aged Youth.* Los Angeles, CA: Author. Available: http://smhp.psych.ucla.edu. Accessed November 3, 2006.

Children's Mental Health Ontario. (2001). *Evidence-Based Practices for Conduct Disorder in Children and Adolescents.* Toronto: Author.

Connor, D.F. (2002). *Aggression and Antisocial Behavior in Children and Adolescents: Research and Treatment.* New York: Guilford Press.

Ducharme, J.M. (1999). A conceptual model for treatment of externalizing behaviour in acquired brain injury. *Brain Injury, 9,* 645–668.

Ducharme, J.M. (2000). Treatment of maladaptive behavior in acquired brain injury: Remedial approaches in postacute settings. *Clinical Psychology Review, 20* (3), 405–426.

Faraone, S.V. (2003). *Straight Talk about Your Child's Mental Health: What to Do When Something Seems Wrong.* New York: Guilford Press.

Findling, R.L. (2003). Treatment of aggression in children. *Primary Care Companion Journal of Clinical Psychiatry, 5* (supp. 6), 5–9.

Garbarino, J. (1999). *Lost Boys: Why Our Sons Turn Violent and How We Can Save Them.* Toronto: Random House.

Garbarino, J. & deLara, E. (2002). *And Words Can Hurt Forever.* New York: Free Press.

Godel J. (2002). Fetal alcohol syndrome. *Paediatrics & Child Health, 7* (3), 161–174.

Golding, L. (2003). *Resiliency Factors in Violence Prevention.* Unpublished master's paper, York University, Toronto.

Greene, R.W. (2001). *The Explosive Child: A New Approach for Understanding and Parenting Easily Frustrated, Chronically Inflexible Children.* New York: HarperCollins.

Hospital for Sick Children. Cyber-bullying. *About Kids Health.* Toronto: Author. Available: www.aboutkidshealth.ca/ofhc/news/Other/3879.asp. Accessed November 3, 2006.

Jenkins, J. M. & Keating, D. (1998). *Risk and Resilience in Six- and Ten-Year-Old Children.* Hull, QC: Human Resources Development Canada.

John Howard Society of Alberta. (2001). *Gangs.* Available: www.johnhoward.ab.ca/PUB/gangs.htm. Accessed November 3, 2006.

Keenan, K. (2002). The development and socialization of aggression during the first five years of life. In R.E. Tremblay, R.G. Barr & R.deV. Peters (Eds.), *Encyclopedia on Early Childhood Development.* Montreal, QC: Centre of Excellence for Early Childhood Development.

Law, M., Kapur, A. & Collishaw, N. (2004). *Health Promotion in Canada 1974–2004: Lessons Learned.* Ottawa: Office for Public Health, Canadian Medical Association.

Levant, R.F. (2001). The crisis of boyhood. In G.R. Brooks & G.E. Good (Eds.), *The New Handbook of Psychotherapy and Counseling with Men, Volume 1* (pp. 355–368). San Francisco, CA: Jossey-Bass.

Liquor Control Board of Ontario. (2005). *Safe Proms: Binge-Drinking Facts.* Available: www.lcbo.com/socialresponsibility/bingedrinking.shtml. Accessed November 6, 2006.

MacKay, S., Henderson, J., Root, C., Warling, D., Gilbert, K.B. & Johnstone, J. (2004). *TAPP-C: Clinician's Manual for Preventing and Treating Juvenile Fire Involvement.* Toronto: Centre for Addiction and Mental Health.

Malone, R.P., Delaney, M.A. & Sheikh, R. (2004). How to reduce aggression in youths with conduct disorder. *Current Psychiatry Online, 3* (4). Available: www.currentpsychiatry.com/pages_backIssues.asp. Accessed November 6, 2006.

Mash, E.J. & Wolfe, D.A. (2005). *Abnormal Child Psychology* (3rd ed.). Belmont, CA: Wadsworth/Thomson Learning.

McIntyre, T. (2005). *Teaching Social Skills to Kids Who Don't Have Them.* Available: http://maxweber.hunter.cuny.edu/pub/eres/EDSPC715_MCINTYRE/SocialSkills.html. Accessed November 6, 2006.

McNamee, J.E. & Offord, D.R. (1994). Prevention of suicide. In *Canadian Task Force on the Periodic Health Examination* (pp. 456–467). Ottawa: Health Canada.

Miedzian, M. (1991). *Boys Will Be Boys: Breaking the Link between Masculinity and Violence.* New York: Anchor Books/Doubleday.

Moeller, T.G. (2001). *Youth Aggression and Violence: A Psychological Approach.* Mahwah, NJ: Lawrence Erlbaum.

New South Wales Department of Community Services. (2003). *Discussion Paper on the Development of Aggressive Behaviour in Children and Youth: Implications for Social Policy, Service Provision, and Further Research.* Ashfield, NSW, Australia: Author.

Office of the Surgeon General. U.S. Department of Health and Human Services. (2001). *Youth Violence: A Report of the Surgeon General.* Washington, DC: Author.

Pederson, P.B., Draguns, J.G., Lonner, W.J. & Trimble, J.E. (Eds.). (2002). *Counselling Across Cultures* (5th ed.). Thousand Oaks, CA: Sage.

Pepler, D.J. & Craig, W. (1996). *A Developmental Profile of Risks for Aggressive Girls.* Unpublished. Toronto.

Potegal, M. & Archer, J. (2004). Sex differences in childhood anger and aggression. *Child and Adolescent Psychiatric Clinics of North America, 13,* 513–528.

Quinsey, V.L., Skilling, T.A., Lalumière, M.L. & Craig, W.M. (2004). *Juvenile Delinquency: Understanding Individual Differences.* Washington, DC: American Psychological Association.

Raphael, D. (2003, March). Addressing the social determinants of health in Canada: Bridging the gap between research findings and public policy. *Policy Options,* 35–40.

Richard Weiler and Associates. (1994). *Youth Violence and Youth Gangs: Responding to Community Concerns.* Ottawa: Federation of Canadian Municipalities.

Rickert, V.J. & Weimann, C.M. (1998). Date rape among adolescents and young adults. *Journal of Pediatric and Adolescent Gynecology, 11,* 167–175.

Sexton, T.L. & Alexander, J.F. (2000, December). Functional family therapy. *Juvenile Justice Bulletin,* 1–7.

Shamsie, J., Lawrence, J. & Hood, C. (Eds.). (2003). *Antisocial and Violent Youth, Volume II.* Toronto: Centre for Addiction and Mental Health.

Shamsie, J., Nicholl, S. & Madsen, K.C. (Eds.). (1999). *Antisocial and Violent Youth: The Latest Research of Over 600 Authorities in an Easy-to-Read Format.* Toronto: Lugus Publications and the Institute for the Study of Antisocial Behaviour in Youth.

Simmons, R. (2002). *Odd Girl Out: The Hidden Culture of Aggression in Girls.* Orlando, FL: Harcourt.

Statistics Canada. (2004). *National Longitudinal Survey of Children and Youth.* Ottawa: Author.

Substance Abuse and Mental Health Services Administration. (2001). *The CMHS Approach to Enhancing Youth Resilience and Preventing Youth Violence in Schools and Communities.* Rockville, MD: Center for Mental Health Services.

Substance Abuse and Mental Health Services Administration. (n.d.). *The Olweus Bullying Prevention Program.* SAMHSA Model Programs. Washington, DC: Center for Substance Abuse Prevention.

Sullivan, K., Cleary, M. & Sullivan, G. (1994). *Bullying in Secondary Schools: What It Looks Like and How to Manage It.* London, UK: Paul Chapman.

Tremblay, R.E. (2002). Prevention of injury by early socialization of aggressive behavior. *Injury Prevention, 8* (Suppl. 4), 17–21.

Tremblay, R.E., Nagin, D.S., Seguin, J.R., Zoccolillo, M., Zelazo, P.D., Boivin, M. et al. (2004). Physical aggression during early childhood: Trajectories and predictors. *Pediatrics, 114* (1), 43–50.

Underwood, M.K. (2003). *Social Aggression Among Girls.* New York: Guilford Press.

Resources

The Canadian Safe School Network
CSSN works to reduce youth violence through various initiatives.
www.canadiansafeschools.com

Child and Youth Friendly Ottawa
This site contains links to several anti-bullying initiatives.
www.youthottawa.ca

The Fourth R: Strategies for Healthy Youth Relationships
This Canadian school program aims to build healthy school environments
by promoting healthy relationships (the "fourth R") among young people.
The program focuses on many forms of aggression, including dating violence,
bullying, peer violence and group violence.
www.youthrelationships.org

Keep Schools Safe: The School Safety and Security Resource
This American site offers information on safety- and aggression-related issues
for students, parents, teachers and other school staff.
www.keepschoolssafe.org/kss/school-safety/school-violence/

Kids Help Phone
Counsellors respond to phone and online questions from young people across
Canada 24 hours a day, 365 days a year. Counsellors provide immediate support
as well as referrals. Kids Help Phone also has student ambassador and public
education programs.
1 800 668-6868
www.kidshelpphone.ca

NYU Child Study Center
This American website offers children's mental health information for child mental
health professionals, front-line workers, and parents and families.
www.aboutourkids.org

Youth Violence: A Report of the Surgeon General
Chapter 4 of this report by the U.S. Surgeon General discusses risk and protective
factors for youth aggression.
www.surgeongeneral.gov/library/youthviolence/chapter4/sec2.htmls